Toward Next-Generation Performance Budgeting

DIRECTIONS IN DEVELOPMENT
Public Sector Governance

Toward Next-Generation Performance Budgeting

Lessons from the Experiences of Seven Reforming Countries

Donald Moynihan and Ivor Beazley

Contents

Box

Figures

Tables

About the Authors

Ivor Beazley is a senior public sector specialist at the World Bank who currently focuses on public finance management issues in Europe and Central Asia. He is a development professional with 25 years of practical experience with implementing financial management reforms in governments and state-owned enterprises around the world. He has worked at the World Bank since 2003 and was previously deputy head of the Governance Department at the U.K. Department for International Development. He is qualified as a chartered accountant in the United Kingdom and is a graduate of Cambridge University.

Donald Moynihan is the Epstein Professor of Public Affairs at the La Follette School of Public Affairs, University of Wisconsin-Madison. His research on public sector organizational performance has won awards from the Academy of Management, the American Political Science Association, the Association of Public Policy and Management, and the American Society for Public Administration. His book, *The Dynamics of Performance Management: Constructing Information and Reform*, was named best book by the Academy of Management's Public and Nonprofit Division and received the Herbert Simon award from the American Political Science Association. He is currently the president of the Public Management Research Association.

Maarten de Jong is a budget specialist with the Netherlands Ministry of Finance tasked with budgetary reform and oversight. He has also provided technical assistance and has done research on budget reforms in Eastern Europe, Asia, and North Africa on behalf of, among others, the Netherlands government, the Organisation for Economic Co-operation and Development, the European Commission, and Ernst and Young. He earned a PhD in public administration from Erasmus University, Rotterdam, for research on the use of performance information for budgetary purposes by public sector agencies in the United States and the Netherlands. His work has been published in a number of international publications, among them *Public Administration Review* and the *OECD Journal on Budgeting*.

Lewis Hawke has headed the Public Expenditure and Financial Accountability (PEFA) Secretariat since November 2014; PEFA is a global, multidonor initiative for assessing public financial management that has been used in more than 140 countries. Previously he was a lead public sector specialist for the World Bank in Europe and Central Asia. He has worked on public sector management and international development for more than three decades and in more than 30 countries; for about 20 years he was a senior official in the Australian Government Department of Finance and the U.K. Treasury managing leading-edge public administration reforms. He has contributed to books and has published journal articles on public sector management issues and has academic qualification in economics, accounting, and business management. He is a Lifetime Fellow of the Institute of Public Administration of Australia.

Frank Mordacq, who has a master's degree in public law, has since 2011 been chief of the Budgetary and Accounting Service of the French Ministry of Finance. Except for a two-year period (1990–92) when he was financial attaché to France's permanent Mission to the United Nations, he has been with the Ministry since 1985. In March 2003 he was appointed to head the new Budgetary Reform Branch, and in 2006 became director general of the Modernization of the State Branch, which is charged with coordinating and assisting all levels of administration with modernization. The Branch brings together a variety of initiatives related to implementing new management policy. He has written three books directly related to the topic of this volume.

Ringa Raudla is a professor of public finance and governance at Ragnar Nurkse School of Innovation and Governance, Tallinn University of Technology, Estonia. Her main research interests are fiscal governance, public budgeting, institutional economics, and public management reforms. She has also worked as a consultant for various governmental organizations, including the Ministry of Finance and the National Audit Office in Estonia. Among her recent publications are articles in *Public Administration Review, Governance, Journal of Public Policy*, and *Public Administration*.

Ekaterina Vaksova has for more than 15 years been a consultant on public finance management, specifically performance budgeting, fiscal federalism, interbudgetary relations, and budget methodology. Previously she worked for more than 10 years as deputy general director of the Research Budgetary Center, a Russian nongovernmental organization. In the course of her career she has drafted normative and methodological acts for the Russian Ministry of Finance and other state executive bodies, analyzed international and local experience to identify the best practice examples, and trained civil servants. Since 2001, she has been a consultant to the World Bank and other international organizations such as the U.K. Department for International Development, United Nations Development Programme, and the Technical Aid to the Commonwealth of Independent States.

Acknowledgments

This study was prepared by Donald Moynihan of the University of Wisconsin–Madison, and Ivor Beazley of the World Bank. Country case studies were prepared by Lewis Hawke, head of the PEFA Secretariat and former official of the Australian Ministry of Finance (Australia); Maarten de Jong of the Netherlands Ministry of Finance and Erasmus University (Netherlands and Poland); Ringa Raudla of the Tallinn University of Technology (Estonia); Frank Mordacq, former official of the French Ministry of Finance (France); Ekaterina Vaksova, consultant (the Russian Federation); and Donald Moynihan (United States). The authors are grateful to the governments of Australia, Estonia, France, the Netherlands, Poland, the Russian Federation, and the United States for participating in the study and for their comments and contributions to the country case studies.

The authors also thank Allen Schick of the University of Maryland; Teresa Curristine of the IMF Fiscal Affairs Department; Neil Cole of the Collaborative Africa Budget Reform Initiative; Nicola Smithers, World Bank Global Lead for Budget; and Mark Ahern, World Bank Lead Public Sector Specialist, for providing valuable insights for the study.

The authors also thank the Ministry of Finance of Russia for generously financing the study.

Abbreviations

ANAO	Australian National Audit Office
APP	annual performance plan, France
APR	annual performance report, France
ATP	Agency Targeted Programs, the Russian Federation
BOP	Program Operating Budget (*Budget Opérationnel de Programme*), France
CBA	Central Budget Authority, France
CIAP	Inter-ministerial Program Audit Committee (*Le Comité interministériel d'audit des programmes*), France
COO	chief operating officer
CPM	Chancellery of the Prime Minister, Poland
DOF	Department of Finance, Australia
ECA	Eastern Europe and Central Asia
ENA	Ecole Nationale d'Administration
EU	European Union
FEAD	Financial and Economic Affairs Directorate, the Netherlands
FMIP	Financial Management Improvement Program, Australia
FTP	Federal Targeted Program, the Russian Federation
GAO	Government Accountability Office, United States
GPRA	Government Performance and Results Act of 1993, United States
ICT	information and communications technology
IMF	International Monetary Fund
IT	information technology
LOLF	Organic Financial Law (*loi organique relative aux lois de finances*), France
MILOLF	Commission Monitoring LOLF Activity (*Mission d'Information Relative à La Mise En Œuvre De La Loi Organique Relative Aux Lois De Finances*), France
MNE	Ministry of National Education, Poland
MOED	Ministry of Economic Development, the Russian Federation

MoF	Ministry of Finance
MP	Member of Parliament
MRD	Ministry of Regional Development, Poland
MYFP	Multi-Year Financial Plan, Poland
NAO	National Audit Office, Estonia
NCLB	No Child Left Behind Act, United States
NDS	National Development Strategy 2020, Poland
OECD	Organisation for Economic Co-operation and Development
OMB	Office of Management and Budget, United States
OPM	Office of Personnel Management, United States
PART	Program Assessment Rating Tool, United States
PB	performance budgeting
PFP	pay-for-performance, Estonia
PFRD	Public Finance Reform Department, Ministry of Finance, Poland
PGPA	Act Public Governance, Performance and Accountability Act 2013, Australia
PIO	Performance Improvement Officer, United States
PPBS	Planning Programming Budgeting System
PPP	public-private partnership
RCB	Planning, Programming, and Budgeting System (*Rationalisation des choix budgétaires*), France
SBS	State Budget Strategy, Estonia
SOAR	Strategic Objectives Annual Review, United States
VBTB	Policy Budgets and Policy Accountability (*Van Beleidsbegroting tot Beleidsverantwoording*), the Netherlands

Overview

Governments around the world have shown sustained interest in improving the efficiency and effectiveness of public spending and in heightening the transparency of and accountability for how public funds are used (Curristine 2006; Schick 2014). Starting with early efforts to introduce program budgeting in the United States in the 1960s, the idea of linking budget allocations and management to results, both within and outside the annual budget process, has gradually gained momentum. In the 1990s, Australia, New Zealand, the United Kingdom, and the Netherlands set off a second wave of performance-oriented budget reforms, which were heavily influenced by new public management theory (Robinson and Brumby 2005). The past 10 years have seen many more countries, often middle- and lower-income, either adopt performance budgeting or commit to the idea. Meanwhile, early adopters such as the United States, Australia, and the Netherlands have begun to overhaul their approaches.

This report examines lessons from performance budgeting in Australia, Estonia, France, the Netherlands, Poland, the Russian Federation, and the United States. A sober look at their experience makes it hard to avoid the conclusion that it is time to rethink what purposes it serves and how to customize approaches to each unique country context. These countries reflect the global interest and the practical difficulties that have to be overcome in moving to performance budgeting; they also offer lessons about how to do it better. Low- and middle-income countries, encouraged by external stakeholders such as donors as well as their own ambitions, may be tempted to adopt textbook models that reflect the promise of performance budgeting but not the actual experience. When performance budgeting does not meet expectations, disappointment is inevitable. Counseling countries to stop trying to link budgeting to performance does not work. Indeed, the sheer persistence of performance budgeting proves that such counsel falls on deaf ears (Schick 2014). Instead, this report offers a path to the next generation of performance budgeting—one that is hopefully both realistic in ambition and useful in practice.

Performance budgeting has a deep and enduring appeal in that it promises to improve public sector performance through transparency, a better distribution of resources, and careful management (Curristine 2005). What government would not want to allocate resources in a way that fosters efficiency, effectiveness, transparency, and accountability? However, normative aspirations are poor predictors of how performance data are actually used. Faith in performance budgeting is sustained by a willingness to forget past negative experiences and assume that this time reform will be different. The gap between promise and practice gives rise to a series of ironies: while performance budgeting promises evidence-based decision-making, the evidence to support its adoption is weak; while it seeks to increase organizational learning, as yet little has been learned about what make these systems more or less successful over time; while it demands objective evidence of improved performance, evidence of its own effectiveness is questionable. Without a significant re-evaluation, performance budgeting's history of disappointment seems likely also to be its future.

Country reporting requirements tend to be similar, this study found, with performance data tied to the budget reporting process. The results of such requirements have also tended to be similar: performance data may appear in the budget but have little impact on budget allocation decisions. However, the general pattern of disappointment masks real variations both in how countries have undertaken performance budgeting and in benefits that have arisen outside the budget process. These variations offer clues for how to build a model of next-generation performance budgeting (table O.1). A starting point is to examine the gap between the classic pitfalls that face new or even experienced adopters and how those who have used it longest and somewhat effectively have modified their expectations. In this study Australia, the Netherlands, and the United States are clearly in the latter group.

A next-generation approach recognizes that not only are the transaction costs of meeting governmentwide reporting requirements significant, they often result in a checklist mentality. A more targeted approach that ties performance data to service delivery goals can both reduce administrative costs and make performance data more useful. It requires systematic differentiation between ministries and programs that merit a substantial performance focus and those where a lighter regime is appropriate.

The experience with performance budgeting suggests that its impact on how annual budgets allocate resources has been minimal. During a budget crisis, governments tend to revert to giving inputs precedence and largely disregard program and performance data. The annual budget timetable is too compressed for good analysis of program quality, given the often complex connection between spending and results. Other activities are better suited to using performance data to ask and answer nuanced performance questions: program evaluations are better at providing evidence of whether a program is working; learning forums are better at using performance data to inform management decisions; and spending reviews are better at assessing the value of public spending. Performance budgeting can, with some justification, be better

Table O.1 Toward Next-Generation Performance Budgeting

Question	Classic pitfalls	Next generation
Where to start?	Requirements for reporting on governmentwide budget performance that are formalistic, onerous, and rarely met	A differentiated approach that emphasizes the most crucial service delivery areas and strategic policy priorities
What are the expectations?	The budget process as the main engine of a governmentwide effort to introduce performance-based management	Changes to the budget process as one part of a comprehensive performance management toolkit, aimed at changing attitudes and incentives in the public sector. Incremental change in step with other reforms that support performance orientation.
When and where are performance data used?	In theory, when the budget is prepared and at year-end, though rarely in practice	At multiple decision points, not just during budgeting but also in management and policy routines throughout the year, such as periodic spending reviews
Who are the most likely users?	Budget officials	Program managers in line ministries
What administrative capacities are needed?	Assumes that administrative capacities and norms are in place, although often there are considerable administrative deficiencies	Seeks to make performance budgeting consistent with contextual capacities and needs; performance data cannot create the capacities necessary for their effective use
What is the timeline for change?	Short-term approach: prioritizes an individual reform initiative, which will often be abandoned, to be replaced by something similar	Long-term approach: values consistency across multiple reform efforts and incremental adaptive change on the basis of experience

promoted as a tool for increasing accountability and transparency, as long as there is careful management of the risks of selective, or manipulative, use of performance data.

Institutional support and expectations for performance budgeting often vary both across and within countries, and the systems need to be matched realistically to contextual capacities. The countries that have most modified their approaches are ones that already had considerable administrative capacity in such areas as accounting, personnel management, and strategic planning. Yet, even they have sought to reduce the transaction costs that arise from performance budgeting. Countries with less administrative capacity should be cautious about overloading their administrators with new demands.

What performance budgeting means has been evolving over time (Schick 2014) and from place to place. Because the concept is so subjective, it is all the more important that policymakers take the time to define their goals and expectations for it and to constantly communicate these (see table O.1). Indeed, a central point in this report is that in practice the line between performance budgeting and performance management[1] is blurring in a way that reflects the limits of how performance data can be used in the budget process but also how they might be used for other management purposes.

Toward Next-Generation Performance Budgeting • http://dx.doi.org/10.1596/978-1-4648-0954-5

The countries that appear to have made the greatest progress are those that were willing to adapt rather than abandon performance budgeting. They have made critical assessments from past experience that have informed incremental rather than dramatic change. This approach acknowledges when problems are occurring and avoids dogged implementation of a system most have little faith in. It also resists the temptation to engage in wholesale change with every new government. If performance budgeting is to establish credibility, some continuity is vital. The adoption, abandonment, and re-adoption of generic one-size-fits-all frameworks should give way to a more iterative and adaptive approach consistent with local goals, culture, and capacities (World Bank 2012). How public officials make use of performance data will not change quickly; nor will their use take root in the course of a single administration. For performance budgeting, success depends on winning the hearts and minds of public officials, not just changing how they report information. That requires a long-term perspective.

An isolated initiative, reforming only the budget process, is unlikely to be successful unless there are also reforms to encourage public sector managers to pay attention to performance and results. Human resource management systems may need to be adapted to link career progress and rewards to results. Auditing, monitoring, and evaluation systems may need to be reoriented to give priority to program results. More profoundly, these reforms normally demand that public servants acquire new skills and behaviors. If these run counter to the prevailing administrative culture, the result may be failure. Political leadership may be required to change the culture, which may depend on sustained efforts over a considerable length of time.

The need to learn from experience and to manage the cultural transition were among 10 findings that emerged from this analysis (table O.2). The findings identified common challenges that some countries encountered and that others are likely to encounter if they are to adopt or update a performance budgeting system.

Table O.2 Ten Challenges for Performance Budgeting

1. *Setting Objectives:* Performance budgeting reforms are driven by a variety of motivations and, depending on the political and administrative context, may evoke different responses. For countries with strong centralized governments, the primary objective is typically to make the budget more responsive to national goals and policy priorities. Other countries see it as giving managers more flexibility to allocate resources and innovate to improve service delivery. A primary challenge for governments is to decide explicitly what they want performance budgeting to achieve.

2. *Looking Beyond the Budget:* The annual budget process is too compressed to allow for considered assessment of program performance. Managers are the most likely users of performance information; zeroing in on the budget process understates the value of performance budgeting for managing programs.

3. *Capacity Constraints:* Governments often underestimate how much administrative and analytical capacity is necessary to operate a performance budgeting system successfully. Even OECD countries rarely set aside enough resources, and many countries may lack the capacity for the type of ambitious approach they adopt. Not only should more attention be paid to capacity, but performance budgeting reform may also need to be simplified.

4. *Information Overload:* Countries typically produce too many metrics, leading to information overload. The complexity of programs and indicators must be tightly controlled.

table continues next page

Table O.2 Ten Challenges for Performance Budgeting *(continued)*

5. *Prioritizing Strategic Goals:* Different performance data serve different needs; metrics for the most salient service delivery areas are more likely to be used.

6. *Managing Performance Perversity:* Too much emphasis on performance can motivate gaming behavior. Manipulation of performance data is rare, but when it comes to light it can create severe trust and legitimacy problems for governments.

7. *Routinizing Performance Information Use:* Building separate program evaluation, audit, and learning routines can address policy and management questions and provide valuable complements to performance budgeting.

8. *Changing Behavior:* Changing public employee attitudes is difficult. It takes persistent efforts, often over a decade or more, to introduce a performance-oriented culture, supported by general public service reforms. The pace and ambition of changes should reflect this reality.

9. *Balancing Political and Bureaucratic Support:* A political champion can help direct attention to performance budgeting—but it can also create opposition and abandonment if reform is viewed as a partisan tool.

10. *Learning from Experience:* The countries that have progressed most have done so by identifying and resolving the shortcomings of previous reform efforts, rather than repeating past failures or starting anew.

Note

1. Moynihan (2008, 5) defines performance management as "a system that generates performance information through strategic planning and performance measurement routines, and connects this information to decision venues, where, ideally, the information influences a range of possible decisions."

Bibliography

Curristine, Teresa. 2005. "Performance Information in the Budget Process: Results of the OECD 2005 Questionnaire." *OECD Journal on Budgeting* 5 (2): 87–131.

Moynihan, Donald P. 2008. *The Dynamics of Performance Management: Constructing Information and Reform.* Washington, DC: Georgetown University Press.

Robinson, Marc, and Jim Brumby. 2005. "Does Performance Budgeting Work? An Analytical Review of the Empirical Literature." IMF Working Paper WP/05/210, International Monetary Fund, Washington, DC. https://www.imf.org/external/pubs /ft/wp/2005/wp05210.pdf.

Schick, Allen. 2014. "The Metamorphoses of Performance Budgeting." *OECD Journal on Budgeting* 13 (2): 49–79.

World Bank. 2012. *The World Bank Approach to Public Sector Management 2011–2020: Better Results from Public Sector Institutions.* Washington, DC: World Bank.

PART I

Analysis

CHAPTER 1

Getting Started

Introduction

This study was initiated by the World Bank in response to sustained interest on the part of budget officials in Eastern Europe and Central Asia (ECA) to learn more about the experiences of OECD countries and other governments in the region in implementing performance budgeting. Rather than learning about theory and best practice, budget officials wanted to know more about the practical challenges and how countries had adapted their approaches to their own context. Many countries in the ECA region have moved to performance budgeting but most have made limited progress.

All performance budgeting efforts have a common goal—to focus the mindset and behavior of public officials on policy priorities and results. It is confusing, however, that there is no standard blueprint for these reforms, which may be referred to as *results-based budgeting, program budgeting, performance-informed budgeting,* or some other moniker. This report uses the term *performance budgeting* to refer to all the variants, but distinguishes it from such techniques as program evaluations and spending reviews. While a strict definition of performance budgeting implies a direct relationship between performance data and budget decisions, it is more realistic to recognize it as the provision of performance data about public services, for example, "a performance budget is any budget that represents information on what agencies have done or expect to do with the money provided to them" (Schick 2003, 201).

The findings are presented as a series of lessons that emerge from the cases studied; the full case studies can be found in part II, chapters 5–11. In each case the focus is on the national government, although state and local governments also use performance budgeting techniques. Efforts to systematically and critically compare the performance systems of different countries are relatively rare, and the research design choices for this study were deliberately intended to generate realistic insights based on capturing aspects of implementation that a purely survey-based approach cannot identify.

The countries selected as case studies have been using performance budgeting for varying amounts of time. For example, Australia, France, the Netherlands, and the United States have been revising their approach over decades but Poland, Estonia, and the Russian Federation are relatively recent adopters. The selection makes it possible to gain insights into how performance budgeting reforms evolve over time, and what newer adopters can learn from more seasoned users. For each country an expert with comprehensive knowledge of its performance processes was selected to write a detailed report, guided by a set of standard questions to make comparisons easier (see the appendix for the questionnaire). For quality assurance, case descriptions were also reviewed by government officials and the editors. In structuring the case design, experts were asked not only to describe the current performance budgeting process and how it was working but also to account for precursors of these systems to gain an understanding of whether countries had engaged in learning over time. The study also tried to ground discussions of how different countries used performance information by reviewing how performance data are used in the same policy area of secondary education.

Setting Objectives

A fundamental problem is that there is no compelling and proven model of how performance should work, which means that policymakers need to identify clear and realistic goals and expectations. Schick (2014, 2) notes the following:

"Despite its well-documented provenance and chequered past, performance budgeting still invokes wonder, as if it were a novel, experimental approach that must be designed anew and explained every time a government attempts to focus budgeting on results. Performance budgeting has had many lives, sufficiently dissimilar from one another to excite the imagination that this time will be different, that the latest iteration will be truly transformative."

Schick's point reflects the malleability of the term *performance budgeting*, which causes confusion about what it really means, unjustified expectations about its impact, and excessive demands on the traditional budget process.

There might be hope that research on performance budgeting might help, but in fact it has a record of dashed expectations rather than lessons to be learned (Schick 2014). While there is growing empirical research on the use of performance information (Kroll 2015), the findings have not had much influence on practice. Performance reforms rarely take into account nuanced theories of human behavior (Robinson and Brumby 2005); instead they rely on ideas that are more intuitive: measurement of performance is a good thing, and performance data will foster its use (Van Dooren, Bouckaert, and Halligan 2008). Such an intuitive logic may be reinforced by a success story from another government, even though a new adopter may not recognize, much less adopt, many of the contextual factors that led to the success (World Bank 2012).

In an attempt to analyze what performance budgeting is good for, figure 1.1 quantifies the extent to which the seven countries in this study made use of performance data for different purposes, corresponding to the main perceived benefits of performance budgeting.

Figure 1.1 Use of Performance Data for Management, Budgeting, and Accountability

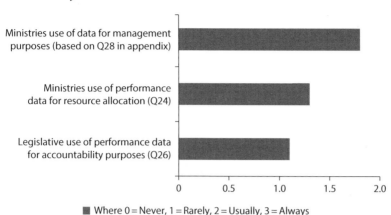

Where 0 = Never, 1 = Rarely, 2 = Usually, 3 = Always

In practice there are some commonalities between countries, but they mostly relate to processes. At least superficially, performance budgeting systems look remarkably similar, incorporating legal requirements for departments and programs to report performance data. The central budget authority (CBA) typically oversees the system, monitoring whether or not data are reported. Usually reporting requirements are annual; identify strategic goals, performance targets, and actual outcomes; and are tied to the budget preparation process. In some cases, the Prime Minister's Office or the Minister of Economic Development may guide the setting of goals and monitoring of progress, and a separate audit agency may verify data quality.

Transparency and Accountability: Such practices establish a baseline for one performance budgeting goal, which is to facilitate transparency and accountability (see figure 1.1). Some countries may be satisfied with making the information available, although in the cases studied policymakers generally hoped that performance data would improve decision making. While making the data available sets a base level of transparency, there is little evidence that the public or politicians use the data systematically to exert control over agencies. Performance data may sometimes be referenced in budget discussions between central and line ministries; more often line ministries use the data to advocate for more resources. In the Netherlands, the CBA tried to resolve this question by asking ministries to determine the degree of control they exerted over policies. The intent was to ward off the tendency of ministries to promise outcomes for policies over which they had only marginal control.

Resource Allocation: Another performance budgeting goal is to make resource allocations more results-oriented. In the countries studied, this goal was rarely met (table 1.1). Country experts usually characterized their systems as "presentational performance budgeting": performance data are presented in the budget, but without a clear or consistent link to decision-making.

While policymakers might demand performance metrics, they seem not to use them at all systematically for resource allocation. In part, this is because it is difficult to attribute causal relationships between spending and performance measures or determine the right response when performance is poor. This basic problem, which occurs in all settings, is not easily solved. In Australia even relatively sophisticated efforts, such as accrual accounting or linking budgets to outcomes, did not resolve the complex problems involved in matching spending with results.

This study's results align with OECD cross-country surveys that have found little evidence of direct links between public expenditures and performance information (Hawkesworth and Klepsvik 2013).[1] Some countries no longer claim they have a strong system. For example, the most recent U.S. and Australian reforms rarely mention performance budgeting as a goal. In the Netherlands, ambitious reforms in 1999–2002 that sought to integrate all financial and performance data into the budget process proved too ambitious and were unwieldy; revisions in 2011–13 retained a program structure in the budget but reduced the detail sought in performance data. France drew similar lessons from its early forays into performance budgeting: while the link to the budget is still important, performance data have been winnowed from the budget document. In Poland, previous reforms set the goal of replacing the existing budget system with a performance budget, but after successive failures the country set a more modest goal of integrating performance data into the traditional budget. Done well, such an approach offers an example to other countries where adopting performance budgeting resulted in the existence of two separate budgets. While Estonia put a new performance budget in place in 2014, it largely builds upon the basic approach established between 2002 and 2005 rather than a more ambitious framework proposed in 2007.

The budget is, and always will be, an inherently political document, in terms of both partisan politics and the goals and motivations of different government entities. Reformers that aggressively pushed performance data into the budget at the expense of input data in Poland, Australia, the Netherlands, and the United States met resistance from legislators, who instead asked that the data be placed in an appendix or other supplement to input data. Information about inputs is still perceived as the most vital data in annual budget decisions.

The financial crisis of 2008 became a natural experiment on the value of performance data for budgeting. The need to cut spending, but to carefully target the cuts, provided an opportunity to use performance data, but its use to make decisions did not increase (Hawkesworth and Klepsvik 2013). Instead, politicians and finance ministries turned to input data to make difficult spending cuts. During this period the Dutch, Estonian, and French governments started to reduce the amount of performance data in the budget. Rather than performance data informing cuts, decision-makers perceived a tradeoff between performance reporting and the financial information needed to guide resource reductions.

The focus on budget inputs during the financial crisis illustrates a more general finding that the annual budget cycle is too compressed to allow time for rigorous analysis and evaluation of program performance or efficiency. The heart of the budget process is a series of formal routines that have an inherent bias toward incremental change to manage conflict—a bias that is reinforced to the degree that the budget is directed to items that are automatically allocated, such as entitlements or wages. Other tools are better suited to re-aligning expenditures and evaluating spending efficiency and effectiveness, among them program evaluation, expenditure reviews, and management learning forums (see *Routinizing Performance Information Use* in chapter 2).

Strategic Prioritization: While performance budgeting may not influence the budget process, this survey of countries suggests that it is used for setting priorities. Performance budgeting, often the creature of the Prime Minister's Office or the CBA, is used by the center of government to shape decisions within the policy process (see also the section "Prioritizing Strategic Goals"). The administration is interested in results, but those normally come after a political cycle. Immediately after an election, the administration is keen to realign the budget with its political commitments, but support may fade later on, especially if the results do not materialize. Data are also often used for management, as is explored in more detail below.

Looking beyond the Budget

All country experts identified agency program managers as the most likely users of performance data (see table 3). The consistency of these responses across such diverse countries suggests that the results are generalizable. If the most frequent users of performance data are managers, the data are most often used for internal management purposes, such as motivating, goal-setting, and external advocacy (Moynihan 2008).

This finding fits with studies of how performance budgeting works in practice in different countries (De Jong 2013; Moynihan and Kroll 2016; Raudla 2012; Savi and Metsma 2013). An analysis of performance budgeting studies concluded: "Compared with the impact on the legislative stage, the impact of performance budgeting is considerably stronger in the budget execution stage" (Lu, Mohr, and Tat-Kei Ho 2015, 432). Schick (2014, 3) argues that performance budgeting "is increasingly viewed as a subset of performance management rather than simply as a process for spending public money. In contrast to earlier approaches that carved out budgeting as a separate process, it is now widely understood that governments cannot budget for results unless they manage for results."

While in all countries there was an acknowledgment that managers are the most likely users, countries differed in how they responded to this realization. Some countries appeared to intensify their efforts to tighten the connections between data and the budget process, as Russia is doing, but others appear to have decided that a tight link is unlikely and are instead working to facilitate managerial use of data. In Australia, long seen as a performance budgeting leader, new legislation gives more emphasis to on management use of performance data. Rather than imply a direct association between measures and allocations, the revised system instead seeks to better connect performance data with corporate planning for management and accountability purposes, decoupling it from budget processes.

The budget cycle is still an attractive tool for attempting to implement performance reforms because it is often the only predictable, established process that has the attention of all government stakeholders. Continued use of the term "performance budgeting" by finance officials and international organizations reinforces the idea that the primary use of performance data is to inform budget decisions. However, framing reforms as performance budgeting may be misleading, because that prioritizes a domain, the budget process, where performance data are rarely used. Later it becomes all too easy to conclude that, because very little performance budgeting is taking place, the system is having little effect, even though it may be influencing management practices. Framing change more broadly as a performance management approach expands the potential goals and benefits of reform.

Capacity Constraints

To do performance budgeting well requires committing significant administrative resources to creating valid performance data and providing the analytical resources to make use of it. Simply collecting the data and presenting it as a report requires time, effort, and some degree of capacity. It is difficult to fully measure outcomes for any complex public function (Dixit 2002). Administrative staff must find a measure that reflects the underlying goal and that is feasible to collect. The CBA may sometimes review measures to verify that they are consistent with governmental goals, adding another step to the process. Both ministries and CBA staff need to be able to link specific measures to strategic goals. Trying to tie data to the budget requires additional effort. For example, in Poland, where the performance budget is an annex, it takes craft and skill to match performance metrics with budgeted spending items. Actual performance-based analysis requires even more resources; it may never be attended to, or it may come at the expense of other forms of analysis.

Verification of data as reliable depends on there being an independent audit function whose staff can review data sources and how data are collected and investigate any manipulation. In some cases, data collected by a credible third party may lower the costs; for example, Russia relies primarily on its central statistics office rather than on information from ministries. To disseminate data also requires investment in IT systems and in training staff to use them.

To actually make good use of data requires additional analytical capacity. A frequent concern, especially for lower-income countries, is that there simply will not be enough administrative capacity to both design a performance system and analyze its results: there may have to be a tradeoff between creation and use of performance data. Constructing a comprehensive performance reporting system may consume so much administrative capacity that there is relatively little left to analyze what is reported.

Toward Next-Generation Performance Budgeting · http://dx.doi.org/10.1596/978-1-4648-0954-5

In Estonia, ministries regard fulfilling reporting requirements as taking time away from actually analyzing the impact of activities. Even in Australia, which has a relatively sophisticated system, there has been no coordinated, continuing attempt to improve the capacity of public entities to use performance data effectively, which minimizes the effects of reform. In the United States, the degree of effort consumed by Bush-era performance evaluations of all major programs diverted CBA analytical capacities away from traditional policy analysis. At the same time, investment in training for performance management has been declining, even as evidence suggests that such training makes the use of performance data more likely (Kroll and Moynihan 2015). As in the Netherlands, the fiscal crisis meant it was no longer feasible to make the substantive investments in administrative capacity necessary to engage in new comprehensive performance reforms, even as legislators saw policy reviews as having been displaced by the mounds of performance data.

Some countries have accumulated capacity through sheer experience, adapting, for example, accounting and reporting processes to make performance data more understandable. In Australia, the investment in accrual accounting systems improved the quality of performance data. The United States during the Bush administration also directed agencies to prepare budgets to reach performance goals. In their first wave of performance budgeting, the Netherlands and France moved from line-item to program budgets. In all cases, legislators grew concerned about the loss of input information; such efforts were halted in the United States, which reverted to a looser relationship between data and budgets.

One response to perceptions that performance budgeting is burdensome is simplification. In some cases, such as Russia and Poland, performance reporting seems burdensome because departments consider the data to be redundant; those countries would benefit from closer integration of different reporting instruments. In redesigning performance budgeting, the Netherlands and Estonia both reduced duplicative reporting requirements.

Another way ministries might respond to performance budgeting burdens is to seek help from consultants. While appealing, and perhaps necessary in the short run, this approach has shortcomings. A reliance on consultants in Estonia meant that too little attention was paid to the characteristics of that country; it also resulted in a fragmented system as different consultants drew up different aspects of the plan, without much input from those who would implement it (Raudla 2013). Poland benefited from European Union (EU) support for training on performance techniques, but when EU funding disappeared, so did the training. Even in richer countries such as the United States, consultants have been used in ways that foster compliance with reporting requirements rather than enhancing analysis. During the Bush administration, the required performance assessments were often contracted out, resulting in little internal dissemination of knowledge from, or commitment to, the process.

The cost burdens that performance budgeting creates are not always taken into account. Elected officials who see the value of performance data underestimate the transaction costs required to produce them. These burdens could be offset by allowing managers more freedom, but in practice performance reporting rules are added without a proportionate increase in autonomy (Jakobsen and Mortensen 2015; Moynihan 2008). Governments, especially CBAs, are concerned about losing budgetary control on issues like staffing that have long-term budget implications. For example, Dutch managers at first were given significant freedom in hiring, but as a result of stricter controls on organizational costs, authority for hiring staff was moved to a higher level within each ministry.

In short, performance budgeting is not a free lunch; it imposes new administrative processes, and if it is to have meaningful impact it requires regular investment in building analytical capacities. Countries unwilling to invest in the process should expect little return. Rich countries have struggled to strike a balance between their reform ambitions and the resources they actually provide to fulfill those ambitions. The lesson for middle- and low-income countries is to avoid an ambitious governmentwide system that demands significant capacity if that capacity does not exist and is unlikely to be created. Outside advisors or consultants can provide short-term help, but they cannot create the skilled staff, functional reporting, and analytical processes or generate the cultural norms necessary if the benefits are to exceed the costs. The performance budgeting cost-to-benefits ratio becomes more favorable if countries adopt simpler systems and direct them to the most important service functions.

Note

1. Within secondary education, performance data were used more often to monitor, and in some cases fund, schools. A likely reason for this difference is the high political salience of education for citizens, which in turn directs media attention given to rankings of educational performance and political attention to these measures.

Bibliography

De Jong, Maarten. 2013. "Using Performance Metrics in Public Sector Agencies to Learn and Improve: A Matter of Institutional History and Identity?" Paper presented at the Public Management Research Conference, Madison, June 20–22.

Dixit, Avinash. 2002. "Incentives and Organizations in the Public Sector: An Interpretative Review." *Journal of Human Resources* 37 (4): 696–727.

Hawkesworth, Ian, and Knut Klepsvik. 2013. "Budgeting Levers, Strategic Agility and the Use of Performance Budgeting in 2011/12." *OECD Journal on Budgeting* 13 (1): 105–40.

Jakobsen, Mads, and Peter B. Mortensen. 2015. "Rules and the Doctrine of Performance Management." *Public Administration Review* 76 (2): 302–12.

Kroll, Alexander. 2015. "Drivers of Performance Information Use: Systematic Literature Review and Directions for Future Research." *Public Performance and Management Review* 38 (3): 459–86.

Kroll, Alexander, and Donald P. Moynihan. 2015. "Does Training Matter: Evidence from Performance Management Reforms." *Public Administration Review* 75 (3): 411–20.

Lu, Elaine Yi, Zachary Mohr, and Alfred Tat-Kei Ho. 2015. "Taking Stock: Assessing and Improving Performance Budgeting Theory and Practice." *Public Performance & Management Review* 38 (3): 426–58.

Moynihan, Donald P. 2008. *The Dynamics of Performance Management: Constructing Information and Reform.* Washington, DC: Georgetown University Press.

Moynihan, Donald P., and Alexander Kroll. 2016. "Performance Management Routines that Work: An Early Assessment of the GPRA Modernization Act." *Public Administration Review* 76 (2): 314–23.

Raudla, Ringa. 2012. "The Use of Performance Information in Budgetary Decision-Making by Legislators: Is Estonia Any Different?" *Public Administration* 90 (4): 1000–15.

———. 2013. "Pitfalls of Contracting for Policy Advice: Preparing Performance Budgeting Reform in Estonia." *Governance* 26 (4): 605–29.

Robinson, Marc, and Jim Brumby. 2005. "Does Performance Budgeting Work? An Analytical Review of the Empirical Literature." IMF Working Paper WP/05/210, International Monetary Fund, Washington, DC. https://www.imf.org/external/pubs/ft/wp/2005/wp05210.pdf.

Savi, Riin, and Merlilin Metsma. 2013. *Public Sector Reform in Estonia: Views and Experiences from Senior Executives.* Country Report as part of the COCOPS Research Project. http://www.cocops.eu/wp-content/uploads/2013/06/Estonia_WP3-Country-Report.pdf.

Schick, Allen. 2003. "The Performing State: Reflections on an Idea Whose Time Has Come, But Whose Implementation Has Not." *OECD Journal of Budgeting* 3 (2): 71–103.

———. 2014. "The Metamorphoses of Performance Budgeting." *OECD Journal on Budgeting* 13 (2): 49–79.

Van Dooren, Wouter, Geert Bouckaert, and John Halligan. 2015. *Performance Management in the Public Sector.* London, England: Routledge.

World Bank. 2012. *The World Bank Approach to Public Sector Management 2011–2020: Better Results from Public Sector Institutions.* Washington, DC: World Bank.

CHAPTER 2

Day-to-Day Difficulties

Information Overload

Data needs and the usefulness of performance data depend upon the roles and responsibilities of users. What are the right data, and the right amount, differ for a citizen seeking information about a particular service, a manager trying to understand how process changes affect those services, Central Budget Authority (CBA) officials trying to identify the least expensive way to provide services, and elected officials who must make budget decisions. A fundamental challenge for any performance budgeting process is to clarify who are the end users and identify their data needs. A system that aims to be of equal use to elected officials, the CBA, and agency managers will disappoint some, if not all, of them. It will generate too much information, much of which will be viewed as of little value. The challenge is to design a system that satisfies the needs of different users. From the perspective of policymakers engaging with the budget process, one lesson that emerges from the seven countries studied is that where data are concerned, less may be better than more. For instance, it makes more sense for budget officials to give priority to data that relate to allocating resources for the relatively few increments of the budget that are likely to change.

To varying degrees all seven countries experienced the contradictory demands of performance budgeting that gave rise to an excess of budget-related data. Elected officials and the CBA often signal that the value of programs must be communicated in performance metrics, predictably leading to an increase in the number of indicators measured. For example, in the Russian Federation performance reports can run to more than 500 pages, even though legislators see relatively little value in much of the information, and feel overwhelmed and unable to manage the wide variety of measures. Although politicians created the demand for performance data, they suffer from information overload and struggle to make sense of what they receive. Performance data cannot solve basic informational problems: they do not tell policymakers why performance moved up or down, or how to improve it.

Ministries thus receive contradictory signals, sometimes at the same time: policymakers want more data on a wider variety of topics, or new data of better quality, but are frustrated if they get too much. This creates a dynamic where individual programs are encouraged to create more data until there comes a point where a central agency is tasked with reducing the number of metrics. Notably, the three countries in the sample that have been pursuing performance budgeting longest—Australia, the Netherlands, and the United States—have all taken steps to simplify the performance information given to elected officials. Though Australia's recent reforms may actually increase the amount of data created, much of it is channeled into corporate reporting structures for managerial use rather than the budget.

Estonia, Poland, the Netherlands, France, and Russia have reviewed the volume of performance data in the budget with a view to reducing it. Yet even after an effort in 2010–13 to halve the number, Poland still has 5,000–6,000 measures. Between 2007 and 2015 France reduced the number of performance indicators in the budget from 1,173 to 677, giving priority to those that most closely reflect strategic objectives, represent major budget areas, and (to facilitate cross-country benchmarking) are used internationally. In 2011–13 the Netherlands removed about 1,000 performance measures in the budget (about half of the total) but in doing so ran into resistance from line ministries and the Court of Audit. The Dutch CBA, spurred by policy and management goals, emphasized the need to focus on data that policymakers were likely to use. Auditors who valued transparency favored keeping more measures available.

In seeking to reduce the number of measures, the CBA may provide explicit guidance on what constitutes a measure worth including in budget documents; the Russian case study has a detailed discussion of such characteristics, and Australia has a guidance document for ministries. In the Netherlands, ministries are told to include measures where they have strong control over outcomes, making the data more helpful for external accountability or guiding resource decisions (see the following section). In France, ministries have been told that measures must be relevant, auditable, and useful, and they must give precedence to measures that can be used to improve services or reduce costs. Ministries have been encouraged to stop reporting activities or indicators that do not respond to strategic goals or large budget items.

Prioritizing Strategic Goals

One potential benefit of performance information for policymaking is to clarify and direct attention to core policy and service delivery priorities. Such a benefit is less likely where the budget process is the primary or only mechanism for producing results, since the routine nature of budget procedures is unlikely to direct attention to broad questions of policy or service delivery.

Some countries have sought to make clear that not all measures are of equal significance, finding different ways to use performance data to direct attention to the policy goals that are of greatest interest to elected officials and senior managers. In the U.S., agency heads must identify a small number (no more than eight) priority goals that they commit to achieving, and the strategic planning process has been altered to link to the election calendar to increase the political salience of the goals selected. The Netherlands has experimented with a similar approach, focusing annual performance reporting on goals of greatest interest to the ruling parties rather than all possible metrics.

Another form of strategic prioritization is the use of cross-cutting goals. For many strategic goals there is no single ministry that has full oversight of progress toward outcomes, and some countries have therefore attempted to facilitate cooperation between the ministries responsible. In the U.S., the agencies responsible for cross-cutting goals are explicitly identified, and a specific goal leader is assigned to facilitate coordination. As with any attempt to break down bureaucratic fiefdoms, cross-cutting efforts depend upon political support, the commitment of the CBA, and the coordination skills needed to build and facilitate a network.

In prioritizing strategic goals, it helps to clarify whether and how government influences these outcomes. A standard performance budgeting approach is to require all areas of government to identify "outcome" indicators regardless of the degree to which government can control these outcomes. The challenges of a one-size-fits-all approach are most apparent in the case of central policy ministries, such as Ministries of Defense, Economy, and Foreign Affairs, where expenditures typically play a very small part in determining policy success or failure. The Netherlands has sought to add nuance to strategic prioritization by asking ministries to identify the degree to which they control a policy outcome; four distinct levels of involvement are distinguished (see figure 2.1). When government has limited control over the policy outcome, such as homeland security or environmental outcomes, it might seek to stimulate or regulate outcomes. It may also fund services, or directly provide services. In the latter cases, it becomes more reasonable to expect a closer link between resources provided and outputs and outcomes than in cases where government has much less direct involvement in an outcome. Such an approach requires politicians to take a realistic approach to performance data, acknowledging that government does not control outcomes for many services it may have an interest in. This change has discouraged

Figure 2.1 Roles of Government in Executing Policies

Source: Netherlands Ministry of Finance.

Toward Next-Generation Performance Budgeting · http://dx.doi.org/10.1596/978-1-4648-0954-5

ministries from padding budget proposals with performance data that was unnecessary, or seeking to claim credit for tasks they did not really control.

Managing Performance Perversity

In all the countries studied, policymakers generally consider performance data reliable. In some cases, structural changes have been made to make the data more credible. For example, the Netherlands mandated explicit data sourcing and an auditable process of collection so that performance data can be randomly audited. In Poland, continuing efforts to make the data collected more useful may also be bolstering its credibility for policymakers, but their positive attitude is partly a product of the fact that performance data are rarely used to drive decisions, so policymakers have little reason to care about whether they are reliable. There are still some cases, like Russia, where officials may doubt the data produced by ministries themselves and prefer to use other sources.

The general trust in performance data may serve to discount systematic managerial and political risks—risks that the center of government may only dimly understand. The first risk is managerial: that employees will respond defensively to performance requirements they view as punitive. The second risk is political: that the public will respond negatively to instances of data manipulation. The outcome in either case is perverse in that reforms designed to improve performance and trust instead generate gaming and mistrust.

Ministries have a natural preference for presenting data about their successes, but their audience may be more interested in data that reveal failures. While there is a compelling logic for identifying and resolving poor performance, one related risk is that performance data become associated with a punitive framework that employees approach defensively, which undermines the potential for general learning for improvement.

Individuals have been found to be more attentive to negative performance metrics than those showing positive performance (Boyne et al. 2009; Olsen 2015). Thus there may be a negativity bias in how performance data are used, so that poor performance is punished but good performance is ignored. This was apparent in some of the countries studied. In Australia, there have been instances where negative performance results affected funding and organization, and in Poland civil servants see the risks that performance systems bring, but not the potential benefits. In the U.S., the Bush administration's effort to link performance data to funding decisions had limited effect, but programs at risk of budget changes tended to be those that had performed less well (Gilmour and Lewis 2006; Rhee 2014). Some countries may systematically focus on poor performers. Russia's new performance system explicitly targets poor performance, putting programs with low scores at risk of budget cuts and threatening removal of agency heads.

The public may respond negatively not just to stories of performance failure but also to evidence of performance perversity, where ministries or contractors have manipulated data. In most countries, it was possible to identify an example of such behavior, but it was not assumed to be systemic. For example, in the Netherlands, the national rail system altered definitions of delays to improve performance scores. There is also some evidence of manipulation of educational data, although this varies in intensity, from cream-skimming of better-performing students (Estonia), to manipulation of data on student socioeconomic status (Netherlands), to rare examples of systemic cheating (United States).

Perversity carries the risk of serious political damage that may be out of proportion to the real problem: though rare and difficult to identify beforehand, data manipulation has resulted in intense political and media attention and fed public frustration. In the U.S., manipulation of waiting lists for military veterans' health services resulted in the resignation of a member of the Cabinet and significant political criticism of the Obama administration. Most citizens care more about this single example of performance perversity than about the administration's positive performance in other policy areas. This experience closely mirrors controversy about manipulation of hospital waiting times in the United Kingdom (Bevan and Hood 2006).

Because incidents of performance perversity are difficult to predict, few steps are taken to prevent data on them. The risks of data manipulation rise when data are considered important to outcomes, rewards, and allocations, especially if there is a correlation between the performance metric and organizational or individual financial bonuses. Severing the connection between high-powered incentives and imperfect measures reduces the incentive for perversity (Heinrich and Marschke 2010). In the U.S., political and public outrage about the veterans' problem was heightened by a series of warnings by legislative auditors about the reliability of reported hospital wait times. Where there is capacity to audit performance, aggressively responding to such warnings offers another way to minimize perversity and reduce political fallout when it occurs. But many countries may lack independent audit capacity to protect against the risk of data manipulation. Investing in building such capacity should be a priority before suspect performance data may be used to make consequential decisions.

Routinizing Performance Information Use

Performance budgeting is characterized by formal routines to measure performance and disseminate the resulting data, but very little attention is given to establishing routines for use of the data. In most cases, the only formal discussion of performance data tends to occur in reviews of departments by central agencies, perhaps just once a year, and these are usually only a small part of a general discussion of budget allocations. Such routines do not generate serious in-depth exchanges of ideas about how to actually improve performance, or bring together employees and stakeholders involved in different processes.

If the annual budget cycle is too compressed for rigorous analysis and evaluation of program performance or efficiency, more analysis is needed outside that process. However these reviews may be defined, in any setting performance data can enrich the perspectives of policymakers. Performance audits, program evaluations, and program or spending reviews mean different things in different places but commonly reflect venues outside the traditional budget process where performance data can inform assessments of the efficacy of programs.

Spending reviews, as in the Netherlands, tend to be centrally driven. Such reviews can, and should, reflect political and strategic preferences, as well as such factors as the relative magnitude of the function and any related risks. While in some cases they are integrated into the budget process, the growing interest in spending reviews may partly reflect the limits of performance budgeting as a means of assessing the value of public spending.

Program evaluations are generally left to ministries, although evaluation of a program may be required because of outside funding, such as Estonia's EU structural funds, or a comprehensive multiyear schedule, such as that of the Netherlands. For many governments, connecting program evaluations to other performance processes requires a change in practice. For example, while both performance measures and program evaluations deal with the same basic question of how to assess the effects of government action, they often occur in different spheres, using different types of evidence. While the data can tell policymakers about whether performance is holding steady or going up or down, program evaluations can provide insight into what drives performance, why it diverges from targets, and the ultimate impact of program activities on broader outcomes. These complementary types of knowledge can be combined to offer a more comprehensive assessment of outcomes. In Australia program evaluations were seen as especially helpful to complement weak performance data.

The newest innovation in using performance data outside the budget is to support learning forums, data-driven reviews, in which performance data are routinely discussed for management purposes. Such discussions occur, if at all, within organizations and are traditionally driven by such informal factors as the culture and leadership of a department or particular unit. One exception to this pattern is the United States, where recent reforms require quarterly reviews of major performance goals, primarily involving departmental staff but sometimes including other employees and possible stakeholders who could influence how a program is conducted. There, those exposed to quarterly reviews also report higher rates of using performance information (Moynihan and Kroll 2016). The Netherlands also requires policy reviews every four to seven years; in these, ministries answer a set of questions on a given policy area. While the way these reviews are conducted has been questioned, they are intended to provoke internal learning rather than external accountability.

There is a general sense that discussions of performance are now more common than formerly, especially in France, Estonia, and the Netherlands, but there seems to be considerable scope in all seven countries studied for more discussion of how public entities perform. Mandating learning forums, however, runs the risk of disrupting how departments already engage in dialogue about performance or of adding one more formalistic burden to performance systems. This is especially true where the administrative culture discourages open exchanges between different bureaucratic levels. An alternative to mandating

Table 2.1 Principles of Well-Run Learning Forums

Meetings take place regularly.

The emphasis is on meeting important goals.

Agency leaders are demonstrably committed and active.

Engagement of multiple staff levels facilitates learning and problem-solving.

The information considered is appropriate and timely.

There is adequate staff and technological capacity to analyze data.

Quality data—reliable, accurate, valid, comparative, and disaggregated to the most useful level—facilitates analysis.

Issues raised in previous meetings are followed up.

Positive reinforcement is valued.

Feedback is constructive.

Reviews generate similar meetings at lower levels

Source: Adapted from Moynihan and Kroll 2016.

routine assessments of performance data, as suggested by the Estonian case, is to encourage ministries to create their own learning routines and share successful models. Whether learning forums are mandated or voluntary, countries could look for expertise in how to structure them to ensure high quality. The U.S. case offered evidence that the quality of these routines, as reflected in the principles shown in table 2.1, matters to the level of use of performance data (Moynihan and Kroll 2016).

Bibliography

Bevan, Gwyn, and Christopher Hood. 2006. "What's Measured Is What Matters: Targets and Gaming in the English Public Health Care System." *Public Administration* 84 (3): 517–38.

Boyne, George, Oliver James, Peter John, and Nicolai Petrovsky. 2009. "Democracy and Government Performance: Holding Incumbents Accountable in English Local Governments." *Journal of Politics* 71 (4): 1273–84.

Gilmour, John B., and David E. Lewis. 2006. "Assessing Performance Budgeting at OMB: The Influence of Politics, Performance, and Program Size." *Journal of Public Administration Research and Theory* 16 (2): 169–86.

Heinrich, Carolyn J., and Gerald Marschke. 2010. "Incentives and Their Dynamics in Public Sector Performance Management Systems." *Journal of Policy Analysis and Management* 29 (1): 183–208.

Moynihan, Donald P., and Alexander Kroll. 2016. "Performance Management Routines that Work: An Early Assessment of the GPRA Modernization Act." *Public Administration Review* 76 (2): 314–23.

Olsen, Asmus. 2015. "Citizen (Dis)satisfaction: An Experimental Equivalence Framing Study." *Public Administration Review* 75 (3): 469–78.

Rhee, Dong-Young. 2014. "The Impact of Performance Information on Congressional Appropriations." *Public Performance & Management Review* 38 (1): 100–24.

CHAPTER 3

Applying the Results

Changing Behavior

The main goal of performance budgeting efforts in OECD countries has been to support a shift to a performance-based ethos of culture and behavior, where public officials instinctively respond to policy priorities, continuously improve the quality of public services, and seek value for money for the public. While introducing performance budgeting may create the façade of such an ethos, the real question is whether deep underlying beliefs change. To a great degree governments considering performance budgeting must think of themselves as investing in long-term cultural change and professionalization.

One tenet of the conventional wisdom is that unless performance data are tied to the budget process, they will not be taken seriously, and a performance ethos will fail to take hold. Some case evidence aligns with this view. For example, while policymakers in the Russian Federation have expressed concerns about the abundance of new performance reports, the presence of performance data has expanded how policymakers think about socioeconomic development and challenged traditional agency norms, which is a starting point for changing organizational cultures. In France reforms sought to encourage bureaucrats to think not so much of spending constraints alone but to think more of accountability to goals. This has been pursued in part by explicitly identifying managers in charge of key goals, both at the national level, where there are about 80 such managers, and locally, and then by granting them more operational autonomy.

However, there is a risk that too close a link between performance data and the budget may actually limit cultural change. The formality of performance reporting can create a sense of performance as a form of make-work that is separate from management and policy decisions. When performance data actually influence budgets, because the first concern of ministries will still be to protect their budgets, they will view the data as a threat rather than an opportunity to learn. Studies of how information about performance is used in public organizations suggests that the data influence decisions most clearly in organizational cultures that value innovation and a willingness to take risks (Kroll 2015)—traits not generally prized in budget processes. Countries that have pursued performance systems for decades, such as Australia, the Netherlands, and the U.S., have to varying degrees disconnected direct links between performance data and the budget and have looked for other ways to use the data. They are further along in changing their cultures.

Performance reforms themselves depend upon existing cultural norms to be successful. In Poland, the ambitious performance budgeting reforms seemed unrealistic, considering the lack of a performance-oriented culture in much of the public sector, where most civil servants were unaware of the primary goals of the reforms and did not see metrics as an opportunity to learn. Poland also reflects how history can influence the acceptability of reform concepts: The Polish government chose to separate politics and administration as a response to the way communist regimes had controlled both parts of the policy process. Because of that heritage, many of today's bureaucrats view performance reforms as inappropriately blurring the distinction between politics and administration. The exception in Poland is education, where the relevance of test scores and educational reform are generally embraced.

In general, post-communist countries have not been receptive to the notion of tying performance practices to wider performance-oriented reforms, which makes changing the culture more difficult. The struggles of former communist countries with performance reforms illustrate both how much such reforms can contribute to changing cultural norms and how far they still have to go. To a great degree, such reforms are the primary way to communicate to public employees that citizens are owed a reasonable accounting of what their taxes purchase, and that having clear and realistic objectives makes it easier to manage public services. Nevertheless, if the national context does not reinforce such a message, performance budgeting will be seen as a technocratic tool with no connection to how things actually work.

It is difficult to construct a culture that directs attention to performance if that culture does not already exist to some extent in the society. Schick (2014, 7) notes that countries where performance budgeting seems to have worked best already had supportive cultures:

> The unconventional truth is that a performing government depends more on the behavior of politicians and civil servants than on the format of its budget; on managerial skill than on dexterity in measurement; on the professionalism of public employees than on performance bonuses and on other financial incentives.

If officials do not engage constantly with performance data, routines for using performance information will not become institutionalized. How elected officials and organizational leaders allocate resources—including their own time and attention—drives broad cultural assumptions about the importance of outcomes. If personnel systems, contracting practices, or the broader beliefs of public servants are at odds with the idea that results matter, prospects for a performance system will dim.

Performance data will not be used effectively unless the country has a well-trained professional cadre of public servants. If cultural change is moving glacially within the public sector, one path to changing the culture is to change hiring practices to emphasize performance competencies, as the U.S. central personnel office has done. Another path is to incorporate training on performance management into professional schools—the path taken most explicitly by the French. Partnering with universities can open up opportunities for more meaningful training and cultural shaping than is feasible in short on-the-job training opportunities.

Balancing Political and Bureaucratic Support

Ideally, performance budgeting would enjoy strong and broad support from political leaders and bureaucrats alike, but that balance is rarely found in practice. Indeed, political support for reforms more often leads to discontinuity, disruption, and backsliding, making the need for bureaucratic institutionalization all the more important.

Performance budgeting generally relies on a political champion. The growing interest in it in Russia is a good example, since it has benefited from explicit presidential support. But relying on a political sponsor is not risk-free. If political champions disappear or their enthusiasm declines, the system is undermined. For example, in Poland a change in government eroded support for performance budgeting, responsibility for which was shifted away from the Prime Minister's office to the Ministry of Finance (MoF). The Polish experience points to the risk of tying reforms to political sponsors whose fates rise and fall with the election cycle. A new administration has an incentive to criticize or abandon the efforts of its predecessor.

Even if champions remain in office, political opponents may instinctively oppose the systems they put in place. In the U.S., legislative opponents to President Bush distrusted his performance initiatives. Perhaps as a result, President Obama has taken a less visible role in championing such systems; his administration has chosen not to articulate a clear presidential agenda. In France, because performance reforms were associated with the Sarkozy administration, the Hollande administration stalled their expansion and rolled back some pay-for-performance initiatives.

Political champions may have greater success not by directly advocating for the reform but by using political capital to institutionalize it through an inclusive and credible process that cuts across political parties. There are also cases where performance systems have emerged and persisted without an identifiable champion. In Estonia, a performance system has been maintained without overt champions, or even much political interest. Instead reform was pushed by the MoF, which has sometimes been criticized for failing to draw in sufficient political input, and to some extent by pressure from the EU.

The role of the legislature in this process can sometimes be paradoxical. In almost every country performance budgeting was a response to legislative demands for better reporting relating to the budget. The legislature's influence was channeled in transitional countries like Estonia, Poland, and Russia through new organic budget laws and in countries with long experience with performance budgeting, such as Australia and the United States, through legislative amendment of existing practices. In France Parliament pushed for replacement of the centralized financial management controls by a performance-based system anchored in national laws. Yet there is little evidence that legislators regularly use performance data for budgeting or oversight purposes (see table 2.1), even in countries like the U.S. where the legislature has a strong policymaking role.

Perhaps the simplest explanation is that legislators, like other politicians, are eager to endorse performance budgeting initiatives but not interested in using their products, especially when performance-based decisions conflict with the interests of political constituencies. Once adopted, performance budgeting is generally perceived as a technical exercise or a management tool that is therefore subject to executive control and diminishing legislative engagement. Legislative expectations about performance budgeting effects should be realistic—tied to staff willingness and capacity to make use of the data. Even if actual use of the data is minimal, the legislature can take on a more explicit role in evaluating the progress of the performance-budgeting system. For example, in the U.S. the Government Accountability Office, which is attached to the legislature, has periodically assessed how different performance reforms have fared, shaping executive discussions about future directions.

Bureaucratic institutionalization of performance budgeting can override variations in political interest. In the U.S. and France, legislating the performance framework ensured some stability even when political interested ebbed. The Dutch case perhaps best reflects the benefits of bureaucratic institutionalization; there, over time the idea of performance budgeting and the related practices have come to be so generally embraced that it makes relatively little difference whether or not a particular political actor champions the idea. If reforms are to have continuity, during the inevitable periods of limited political interest support must come from elsewhere.

Learning from Experience

A familiar pattern for performance budgeting is as follows: A new administration decides it needs performance-based governance. But more likely than not a predecessor already had such a system. To the extent the old system is considered, it is dismissed as a failure, without any real analysis of why it failed. If the new system is explicitly compared to the old, the intent is to show how markedly different the new approach is. Political incentives intensify the tendency to criticize past administrations. While this may be truer in a presidential or a two party-system than for a coalition government, political dynamics seem universally to encourage some sort of break with the past.

While a new performance reform might be presented as novel and a break with the past, generally the reforms are not all that dissimilar. If one reform failed because of problems with administrative capacity or resistance from a certain set of stakeholders, the new approach is likely to encounter the same problems.

Understanding why performance budgeting has struggled in one period offers vital lessons for subsequent iterations. Countries that adapted such systems effectively did so by learning from their own experience. For performance budgeting, looking carefully at past reforms has three clear benefits: experiential learning, realistic expectations, and gradual cultural change.

Experiential Learning

Organizational learning occurs when processes capture insights generated over time. Governments seeking to learn from their performance budgeting experience usually have plenty of material to work with. In all the countries studied, the current system was not the first one adopted; each had at least one predecessor. In Australia, the Netherlands, the United States, and to a lesser degree Estonia and France, there was evidence of learning from and adapting past performance budgeting processes. Countries that transitioned from communist systems in the 1990s have less experience with newer versions of performance budgeting, although some had predecessors, such as production quotas.

Because experiential learning comes from the same institutional context, it gives reformers an opportunity to adapt a reform in a way that is responsive to that context. For example, while all reforms impose burdens, understanding which reporting burdens were duplicative during one period allows for pragmatic reduction of requirements in a later period, as the Estonian and Dutch cases demonstrate. In Australia, more recent reforms have returned the emphasis to outputs, reflecting a sense that the focus on outcomes in recent years eroded attention to data for management purposes.

More Realistic Expectations

Countries that learned from past performance budgeting efforts tend to have more modest expectations; they do not promise that it will revolutionize governance. In Australia, Estonia, and Poland, for example, the current wave of reforms was explicitly presented as evolutionary compared to more revolutionary previous approaches.

When reforms are based on unrealistic promises, they set themselves up for disappointment. More grounded expectations direct attention to where greater use of performance data can realistically be expected. For example, recent U.S. and Australian reforms have focused explicitly on management use of data. Since every country has only a limited amount of political capital, administrative resources, and bureaucratic energy to invest in reforms, it is important to invest those assets where they will have a larger payoff. In settings where ambitious reform is unrealistic, lessons from experience may serve to encourage more modest and incremental change that is consistent with capacity and cultural limitations.

Gradual Cultural Change

Administrative reforms cannot be instruments of cultural change if reforms are adopted and episodically dropped. If that occurs, employees experience such change as a series of burdensome requirements whose payoffs are disrupted when the reform is dropped; they understandably become cynical about the prospects of a new performance budgeting process.

By drawing lessons from a previous performance budgeting wave in designing another, reformers can communicate a narrative of a continuous general shift in governance, with any particular version of the reform being the next chapter in a long book. However, that narrative is feasible only if there is genuine continuity between reforms and employees can reasonably hope to make progress on problems they encountered before. Cultural change is slow and difficult (Khademian 2002), and those in government need to recognize that it will not happen overnight. But if a change is framed as continuous and cumulative, there is a heightened chance that the norms, beliefs, and behaviors of those operating in the public sector will gradually be altered. Most notably in the Dutch, U.S., and Australian cases, the sense of continuity between reforms has helped to institutionalize a cultural norm related to use of performance data for policy design and management purposes. In Australia in particular, reforms over three decades are clearly connected. While public employees might have frustrations with the latest iteration, there appears to be a permanent shift in values.

What might facilitate learning from past experiences? One possibility is embedding a reform in a statute, especially in a country where statutes are difficult to replace. Reliance on legislation provided continuity in France and the U.S. that had been missing in prior reforms. In both the Netherlands and the U.S. policymakers also benefited from, and encouraged, the intellectual capital of a stable community of experts inside and outside government. Over time a group of Central Budget Authority (CBA) staff provided continuity and an evolving understanding of how the system was working. Audit offices offered a competing view to the CBA, and critiques from academia generated fertile exchanges over the years that both identified problems with the status quo and critiqued specific proposals for addressing the problems.

In the U.S., the CBA has tried to facilitate cross-governmental learning by forming a Performance Improvement Council of agency representatives to share best practices in managing performance. The Dutch, and to a lesser degree the French and Estonian, governments have self-consciously experimented, willing to attempt new approaches and make quick judgments about the outcomes and what needed to be done differently. These included in the Dutch case reducing the amount of performance data reported and better aligning it with coalition priorities, and under the Blair government in the U.K. a Prime Minister's letter that sought to create high-level commitment to specific goals. Between 2007 and 2012 Estonia drafted a concept paper and pursued a series of pilot studies before revising the existing framework. This provided space and opportunity to learn, though the learning was diminished by overreliance on a mix of consultants and a very small team of reformers in the Ministry of Finance who had all gone by 2013.

Bibliography

Khademian, Anne M. 2002. *Working with Culture: The Way the Job Gets Done in Public Programs.* Washington, DC: CQ Press2.

Kroll, Alexander. 2015. "Drivers of Performance Information Use: Systematic Literature Review and Directions for Future Research." *Public Performance and Management Review* 38 (3): 459–86.

Schick, Allen. 2014. "The Metamorphoses of Performance Budgeting." OECD *Journal on Budgeting* 13 (2): 49–79.

Conclusion: Operational Lessons and Key Questions

This report offers some ideas for how performance budgeting could be usefully reconsidered in theory and better institutionalized in practice. Despite its mixed record and some disappointment with it, performance budgeting is still a potent idea. Elected officials and CBAs are never far away from announcing a new iteration of this old idea. Their optimism creates blind spots about the nature of performance budgeting, however, and the difficulties of implementing it. The report concludes by suggesting some practical lessons for governments planning to adopt such a system, and by raising unresolved questions that need to be addressed. The lessons arise partly from the cases reviewed but also from broader experience with implementing significant changes to public financial systems (see box 4.1).

The need to identify a realistic set of expectations gives rise to a specific question: *How do governments measure the success or failure of performance budgeting reforms?* While the inherent logic of performance budgeting is that evidence should matter to decisions, governments are generally reluctant to evaluate carefully whether or not the reforms made a difference, or to rely on high-quality evidence in making decisions. For governments that wish to answer this question, it is much easier to do persuasive evaluations of a reform if information on how it is being conducted is collected in real time, rather than as an afterthought. While determining the ultimate effects of performance budgeting is methodologically difficult, an interim measure of progress is whether public officials are actually using the performance data (Kroll 2015).

Performance budgeting requires changes in how government information is created, analyzed, and communicated, which demands investment in human resource skills. But this insight raises another question: *What investments in capacity matter most for performance budgeting?* In general, governments have not carefully considered how to select employees with skills in data analysis or how to provide training that will improve the use of performance data (Kroll and Moynihan 2015). Relatively little is known about the types of skills or training

---

Box 4.1   Operational Lessons for Performance Budgeting

Identify Clear Objectives for Performance Budgeting: Before initiating a performance budgeting reform, governments should take time to clarify their objectives and expectations. Because performance budgeting is not well-defined, clear objectives will help to guide its design, manage expectations, and increase the chances of success. The objectives should take into account the administrative culture of the country and how civil servants are likely to interpret and respond to such initiatives. Given the many potential benefits that have been claimed for performance budgeting, unless government is mindful of its difficulties and the investments required, ultimately there will be disappointment because reforms will be overambitious and under-supported.

Ensure that Capacity Is in Place for Managing Performance Budgeting: The CBA needs to ensure that line ministries have reliable multiyear budget allocations to plan the delivery of programs. Budget classification and financial reporting systems need to accommodate programs, subprograms, and related planning categories. Where the objective is to devolve greater responsibility and budget authority to program managers, internal controls may need to be revised. Typical constraints on the ability to prepare good performance budgets include separate processes for planning and approval of capital expenditures and the volatility of off-budget donor financing. Ideally, a full accrual-based accounting system would make it possible to match real costs, rather than cash expenditures, to outputs and performance. All these factors need to be taken into account when planning the reform and setting expectations. While the degree to which these factors were present in the cases studied varied, they are often not in place before countries commit to performance budgeting.

Support Performance Budgeting with Other Reforms: Performance budgeting is more likely to succeed when it is part of a broad-based government effort to introduce a more performance-oriented culture rather than being an isolated reform promoted by the CBA. For performance budgeting to work well, human resource management systems need to recognize and encourage good performance; monitoring and evaluation systems need to provide meaningful analysis; data collection and reporting systems need to be timely and reliable; and audit processes need to validate performance reports. Unless broader reforms occur, performance budgeting is likely to be simply a "presentational" approach limited to data creation and dissemination.

Avoid Information Overload: A common tendency when countries introduce performance budgeting is to create a complex architecture of programs, subprograms, and activities, each with its own performance indicators. Countries with the most experience with performance budgeting have steadily reduced the number of programs and indicators over time. This reflects both the administrative burden of reporting and the limited time senior managers have available to monitor performance. The CBA should establish guidelines and do regular vetting to control the proliferation of subprograms and indicators.

Invest in Capacity: Budget analysts typically need new skills to deal with program structures, performance indicators, and the costing of programs. The investment required both in the CBA and line ministries is often underestimated, resulting in inadequate program design, poor quality indicators, inattention to problems, and a passive approach to using data.

---

box continues next page

Box 4.1 Operational Lessons for Performance Budgeting *(continued)*

In addition to classroom training, capacity can also be built through peer learning, so that good practices developed in one area of government can be copied by others.

Where Capacity Is Limited, Start with the Basics: If capacity constraints are significant, governments should consider staged or partial approaches to performance budgeting. Examples are piloting in a few priority ministries or programs, excluding fixed and semifixed costs from the performance budget, and limiting the objectives to simple presentation of the budget in a programmatic form with no attempt to closely link performance data and budget allocation. While program monitoring and evaluation help to create a feedback loop, they are also resource-intensive. At the basic level the CBA should carry out analytical reviews of variances in expenditures and performance. These should be supplemented by more in-depth program evaluation carried out selectively on the basis of criteria such as program size, risk, and political importance.

Differentiate the Approach for Different Parts of Government. Performance metrics are more relevant in some areas of government activity than others and a one-size-fits-all approach can be just a "make work" exercise for some programs. The main factor determining whether performance budgeting is relevant is how close the relationship is between financial resources and policy outcomes. The Netherlands offers an example of such an approach: in its 2014 budget about a third of all programs did not list any indicators. Examples of such programs are those funding counter-terrorism, meteorology, and the financial contribution to the EU. Full performance budgeting should apply to programs where government is the main service provider, such as infrastructure, primary and secondary education, and health.

Routinely Discuss Performance: Performance-based budgets are typically built with a great deal of effort, only to be ignored until year-end. To become relevant, managers need to review and discuss performance reports periodically throughout the year so that necessary course corrections can be made promptly.

Governments need to guard against unrealistic expectations for performance budgeting, and to acknowledge the tradeoffs involved and the investments needed. Governments are too quick to abandon rather than adapt past efforts, and too uncritical of the claimed success stories of others. Still, properly channeled their enthusiasm for performance budgeting can fuel meaningful efforts to improve governance. A starting point is to acknowledge the difficulties associated with performance budgeting. Success depends on both realistic expectations of both its possibilities and what it requires.

---

that will improve the craft of performance budgeting. Some investments in capacity are hinted at in the case studies but deserve more attention. One is the role of IT solutions in reducing the burdens associated with amassing performance data, serving the needs of different users, and facilitating public accountability. IT is potentially a powerful tool, but there is no clear manual for how it might be useful in this case. No country studied could point to an IT approach that has solved basic issues of how to efficiently collect and distribute the appropriate amount of information to each audience.

Toward Next-Generation Performance Budgeting · http://dx.doi.org/10.1596/978-1-4648-0954-5

Administrative culture is clearly important to the success of performance budgeting, but it is pointless to offer a checklist for changing culture, because the levers for change will vary in each setting. Instead, we raise this as a question for future research, in the hope that new performance budgeting systems will be informed by an understanding of the existing culture. Seeking to introduce a culture of performance while looking beyond simple budget reallocations gives rise to another practical question: *Which performance innovations become embedded into the basic routines, practices, and culture of government agencies?* Such a question suggests that governments alter how they look at performance budgeting: rather than treat it as an alternative system that will change how government runs, they can look for ways to make performance data part of processes that are already important but can realistically make use of such information. The budget is primarily a political document, and performance data are more likely to have meaningful influence on policymaking and implementation away from the give and take of political decision-making, in such processes as spending reviews, program evaluations, or ministry learning forums that allow for more nuanced consideration of the meaning and implications of the data. Future research and cross-national discussions of innovations could look at such techniques and seek evidence of how they are actually altering behavior.

Bibliography

Kroll, Alexander. 2015. "Drivers of Performance Information Use: Systematic Literature Review and Directions for Future Research." *Public Performance and Management Review* 38 (3): 459–86.

Kroll, Alexander, and Donald P. Moynihan. 2015. "Does Training Matter: Evidence from Performance Management Reforms." *Public Administration Review* 75 (3): 411–20.

PART 2

Case Studies

CHAPTER 5

Australia

Lewis Hawke

Introduction

Australia has more than 30 years of experience with various adaptations of performance budgeting, most of which can be characterized in OECD terminology as performance-informed budgeting (OECD 2008). Australia has some examples of more explicit resource allocation based on program service volumes and unit costs, but such practices are more prevalent in state governments, because states are responsible for most services, including primary and secondary education, most health care, transport infrastructure and services, and public utilities. The Australian Constitution, adopted in 1901, allocates out responsibility for the various government functions.

At the national level, application of performance-based approaches has been iterative and incremental, although there was a significant change in the late 1990s when accrual-based outcomes and outputs were adopted. This required changes to legislation, regulations, reporting structures, and longstanding conventions about how annual appropriations should be handled. Though since 2013 the changes reflect more an evolution than a revolution, they could have significant effects on how organizational performance is managed.

The approach to performance in the Australian public sector has been periodically refined to adjust the categorization and measurement of performance in ways that are better aligned with the policies and culture of each incoming government. At the same time, the aim has been to address persistent weaknesses in measuring performance, particularly measuring entity contributions to desired policy outcomes.

Performance Budgeting in Australia

The approach to performance budgeting in Australia was in transition in 2015. A new law passed in 2013, the Public Governance, Performance and Accountability Act 2013 (PGPA Act), was the result of consultation by the Department of Finance (DOF) on a wide range of financial management issues over more than a year. The new law not only merged and refined previous financial management laws covering government departments and other entities, it also introduced for the first time the concept of "performance" into legislation affecting public agencies. Previously, agency performance was governed by policy decisions and regulations; general legislative provisions gave the Minister of Finance powers only to issue directions to organizations on finance-related matters.

Creating and Disseminating Performance Data

Some of the new features of performance management introduced through the PGPA Act have not yet been tested because they did not come into force until July 1, 2015. This section describes how those arrangements are intended to operate. Later sections will provide information on the arrangements that have applied until now and how they have evolved.

The new performance framework requires that all entities publish corporate plans and that annual performance statements be linked to corporate plan objectives, to be published in entity annual reports. The annual performance statements will report on progress against plan commitments and performance information presented in portfolio budget statements. At present, portfolio budget statements include detailed information on performance goals for outcomes and programs. These statements are submitted to Parliament when the annual budget is presented for approval. Once the PGPA arrangements are in place, information requirements for the portfolio budget statements will be revised, but as yet there has been no decision about the precise performance information content of those documents.

The clear intention of the changes is to emphasize management and accountability for performance across all entity activities—something largely separate from annual budget plans. The budget retains a link with performance because corporate plans are expected to be framed within entity capabilities, which would include resource constraints. However, any implication that there is a direct association between performance and budget allocation is overborne by greater emphasis on the clarity and transparency of performance goals in corporate plans and accountability for their achievement in annual performance statements. Figure 5.1 illustrates the broad elements of the new approach.

Like Australia's medium-term expenditure framework, corporate plans are intended to cover four years. They must contain six basic elements: an introduction setting out the legal basis and period of coverage; the purpose of the entity; the operating environment; performance proposed to achieve the entity's purpose; capability in terms of workforce, capital investment, and information and communications technology; and risk management.

The performance element of corporate plans is expected to set out clearly how the entity purpose and objectives will be achieved. The DOF suggested approach to presenting this information in corporate plans is illustrated in figure 5.2.

DOF guidance documents (2015a–2015e) detail the types of performance measures that can be used in corporate plans. These documents demonstrate a

Figure 5.1 The New Australian Government Performance Framework

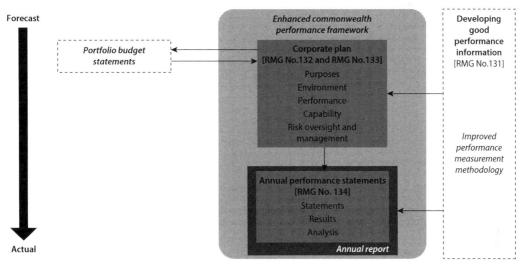

Source: DOF 2015a, 5.

Figure 5.2 A Structured Approach to Presenting Performance Information

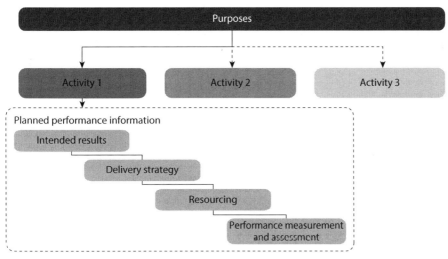

Source: DOF 2015c, 14.

move from the previous approach, focused on a hierarchy of inputs, outputs, programs, and outcomes to one that allows for a wider scope of intended results. This is a return to interest in output information, which had gone out of favor in Australia for a few years. The emphasis in the new guidance documents is largely on establishing a clear logic model that links resources to results; there is a new focus on telling meaningful performance stories, and directing them to the appropriate audiences. The guidance explains that a good performance story is one that demonstrates how effectively the entity's activities fulfil its purpose and how activities might be improved (DOF 2015b).

The new annual performance statements are intended to "provide an assessment of the extent to which an entity has succeeded in achieving its purpose" DOF 2015e, p 4). Content is expected to be directly linked to the performance components of corporate plans, providing details of achievements against stated performance goals and targets. The emphasis is on aligning performance statements with corporate plans and portfolio budget statements (DOF 2015e, 4).[1] The latter will be expected to cover only a subset of the performance information provided in corporate plans. The DOF has not mandated any structures or content for performance statements other than the general PGPA Act broad requirements and related rules. Entities are required to make compliance declarations part of their performance statements, using words to the effect that the information complies with the legal requirements, is based on records properly maintained, and accurately reflects the performance of the entity.

The guidance released to date does not provide any indication of how Parliament or the government will use the performance statements or the corporate plans. There is no suggestion that it has implications for budget discussions or incentives or sanctions linked to performance. If anything, it seems likely that performance information will be increasingly decoupled from budget documentation. The guidance on performance information in portfolio budget statements states that they are intended to relate to particular annual appropriation requests. It further states that portfolio budget statements should contain only a strategically focused subset of performance information reported in the entity's corporate plan, plus any specific measures related to funding for new policy initiatives.

How Is Performance Budgeting Defined?

At the national level in Australia the link between entity performance and budgeting has mainly been general. Annual appropriations for a program or outcome have been associated with objectives, results, and deliverables but rarely tied to a specific quantity or other output. In some instances, resource agreements for demand-driven activities have been negotiated based on unit costs. However, the allocations were not rigidly tied to a specific quantity of services. Unspent funds could be used for other purposes within the program or outcome group, and additional costs were expected to be absorbed without supplementary funding.

Entities have considerable discretion to reallocate funds within broad outcome appropriations, allowing flexibility to move funds between activities with no apparent consequences even if the composition of products changes. Budgets and performance are expected to become even more independent under the new arrangements because the performance information in portfolio budget statements can be less detailed.

The DOF's new guidance on performance information does not define performance budgeting per se. It defines performance in the context of information relating to the efficiency and effectiveness of activities and achievement of an entity's purpose. Performance management is defined as "the use of performance information to monitor and address the fulfilment of purposes" (DOF 2015e, 50). There is no mention of how the budget to contribute to those purposes is determined.

Links with Other Forms of Budgetary Analysis

The new, enhanced performance framework in Australia recognizes that performance indicators are only one means to assess and monitor performance. The guidance states that key performance indicators may not even be the best way to monitor the results of an activity, especially where it is difficult to measure the impact in quantitative terms (DOF 2015a, 9). The guidance documents suggest a range of other tools that can be used, among them benchmarking, stakeholder surveys, peer reviews, and comprehensive evaluations. The evidence for Australian government entities using such methods is very limited and varies according to the extent to which entities consider such methods beneficial in managing their activities and meeting their responsibilities. There is little evidence that the Cabinet considers performance information in budget allocation, except in rare instances where a high-profile program fails, such as the 2010 home insulation program (Commonwealth of Australia 2014). There is more evidence that entities make changes in response to survey, review, and evaluation findings, as reported in their annual reports and identified in the survey.

Program evaluation has not been a formal requirement for Australian government entities since the mid-1990s. In 1987 the Cabinet approved a formal policy of comprehensive evaluation of all major programs within five years (Mackay 2011). The purpose of each evaluation was to examine the extent to which programs were efficient, effective, and appropriate to the original policy objectives. It was expected that the evaluation results would be considered as part of annual budget negotiations and the results presented in annual reports. The quality of evaluations varied considerably, as did their significance for policy decisions and resource allocation. The formal policy was relaxed in 1996 when responsibility for evaluation was devolved entirely to the entities themselves and there was no longer any expectation that results would be considered routinely in budget negotiations.

The Australian National Audit Office (ANAO) has been very active in auditing performance for more than a decade. It has produced over 50 performance audits a year for the last three years. These audits usually focus on the extent to which intended outcomes are being achieved and whether processes can be undertaken more efficiently or effectively (Auditor-General 2014). The emphasis on performance reporting and PGPA Act performance indicators provides a foundation for the Auditor-General to focus on the quality of those indicators. The Auditor-General Act 1997 was amended in 2011 to give the office explicit authority to conduct audits of whether key performance indicators, and the completeness and accuracy of their reporting, are appropriate. This is likely to be an increasing focus for the ANAO in future.

There have been central ad hoc review exercises, generally case by case, in response to government action. From 2006 to 2014 a strategic review initiative identified the highest-priority programs and policy areas for review. The reviews were performed jointly by the DOF and the entities responsible, often with support from external experts. The recommendations for strategic reviews were presented to the Cabinet and considered in the annual budget context. The practice of strategic reviews has recently diminished as the emphasis on reporting performance indicators at the entity level has increased.

In the last decade both conservative (Coalition) and social democratic (Labor) incoming governments have favored the use of broad spending reviews shortly after taking office. Reviews by the incoming Labor administration in 2007 were commonly referred to as "Razor Gang" reviews; the more recent Coalition administration established a National Commission of Audit with a similar purpose but intended to have a broader mandate. Those reviews were more concerned with expenditure savings than with efficiency or effectiveness. They tended to target activities where the policy foundations were more associated with previous governments and therefore likely to be out of step with the policies of the new administration. Although performance information was considered, it is not clear that it had a decisive impact on reallocation of resources.

Changes in Performance Budgeting over Time

The Australian performance framework can be traced directly to a 1983 parliamentary review of government administration (Parliament of Australia 1983). The review, prompted by difficult economic circumstances, highlighted the urgent need for a more efficient and cost-effective public sector. The government's response was to introduce a broad reform that covered many aspects of public administration and encompassed fundamental changes to budgeting and accountability, including introduction of program-based appropriations and medium-term expenditure plans (Parliament of Australia 1984).

The performance agenda was a key component of the Financial Management Improvement Program (FMIP), established as part of the government initiative for reform of public administration. The FMIP was overseen by a cross-agency steering committee and every two years reported to Parliament on progress. A common theme in all the reports, and the Parliamentary review of FMIP in 1990 was the need for better-quality information about performance (Parliament of Australia 1990). Refinements were made to FMIP incrementally to strengthen the use of performance indicators for each program, move toward outcome-focused indicators rather than activities, and introduce a comprehensive program evaluation regime for all budget-funded entities. All programs had to be evaluated within five years and the DOF reviewed the evaluation plans and provided extensive training, support, and monitoring of evaluations.

The change of government in 1996 brought in an administration that was keen to adopt more of a private-sector culture, as was common in other English-speaking countries at the time. The idea that governments could establish a quasi-market for public services defined by fully priced outputs that could be purchased from the source and provided best value for money spawned a revised model for budgeting. The Australian approach drew on New Zealand's output budgeting experience but put more emphasis on outcomes as part of the resource allocation equation. Specific dimensions of performance became mandatory in budget planning, reporting to Parliament, and accounting for results in annual reports. This included outputs by price, quantity, and quality, and outcomes with specific indicators and targets. Evaluation was considered to be part of the responsibility of line entities for delivering quality outputs and outcomes. The central role of the DOF in supporting and monitoring evaluations was discontinued. Legislation and parliamentary procedures were changed to allow appropriations for outcomes and to permit authorization of accrual-based expenses rather than cash.

The new accrual-based outcome and output framework expanded the scope and quantity of performance information substantially. Even so, Parliament continued to be concerned about the quality and relevance of performance information. There was a perception that vital information on input costs had been lost in the transition, and instead outcome information had provided an opportunity for entities to expand their discretion over the use of resources through vaguely worded purposes that could not be measured with any precision. There was also skepticism among parliamentarians about the usefulness of accrual appropriations, which contained charges for the imputed cost of capital and depreciation (Parliament of Australia 2007).

Attempts by the administration to review the appropriateness of output prices and improve the precision of outcome descriptions had little obvious impact. The concept of outputs was eventually dropped in 2010 with the reintroduction of programs that were less comprehensive than the FMIP programs. The new programs were intended to provide a clearer basis for resource allocation and accountability that was more meaningful to stakeholders, especially Parliament. They were also supposed to strengthen the link between government actions and the outcomes they were intended to achieve. The causal link between outputs and outcomes was considered to be more difficult to establish because of the high and broad outcomes approved for use in annual appropriations (Murray 2008).

When the introduction of programs did not effectively address the perceived weaknesses in the performance system, in 2012 the administration embarked on another endeavor to improve the transparency of performance and accountability for results (Australian Government, Department of Finance and Deregulation 2012). The Commonwealth Financial Accountability Review, coordinated by the DOF and Deregulation, involved extensive consultation on a range of issues and reform options, culminating in the PGPA Act.[2]

Adoption of the Current System

The PGPA Act was passed in 2013, in the final months of the outgoing Labor administration. It was subject to relatively little debate in Parliament even though it involved significant changes to the form and content of previous public financial management legislation. It took almost two years for regulations and guidance to be drafted, and it is still too early to comment on their efficacy or impact since very little of the enhanced framework has been implemented.

It is clear that there is a strong emphasis on consistently reporting performance from plans to results. For now, the focus is on establishing reporting structures rather than using the information produced. The guidance implies that the expectations for more extensive evaluation and review anticipated in the PGPA Act will lead to more transparent performance. A further implication is that the expected heightened scrutiny will result in more action to improve performance. It remains to be seen whether this logic will prevail. Experience to date, in Australia and elsewhere, suggests that stronger reporting and accountability measures do not necessarily lead to greater use of performance information, or to better performance. It will be interesting to see how the situation evolves as the new arrangements become fully operational.

Use of Performance Information

Evidence on Governmentwide Use of Performance Information

In 2013 Australian government entities were surveyed to examine perceptions of entity quality and use of performance information. The survey also analyzed factors affecting the quality and use of information.[3] The survey was issued to 90 entities to obtain a balanced cross-section of the population subject to the government's performance information policies at that time; more than half (54) provided complete responses. Follow-up interviews were conducted with 21 respondents to verify and elaborate on the answers. The entities that responded to the survey reflected a reasonable balance in terms of size, functions, legal form, and complexity, and since the distribution was proportionate to the complete population of entities subject to the policies, the survey results can be expected to provide a representative cross-section of the experiences of Australian government entities at the time the survey was conducted.

The main purpose for the development and design of performance information, according to 87 percent of the respondents, was to comply with external requirements, and 71 percent said that performance indicators were identified to monitor operations and assist in identifying areas for improvement. Only 51 percent said that there was serious internal interest in performance information.

Most entities maintained performance management arrangements at the entity and individual levels, but in less than half were the individual and organizational performance indicators closely linked. This suggests that there was little incentive for individuals to contribute to organizational goals.

Entities were asked about the extent to which recipients of their performance information actually used it. About three-quarters indicated that senior management used performance information either substantially or completely. The next most intensive user group within the organizations was business line managers. The least intensive users of performance information were elected officials at only 10 percent and the media at less than 2 percent.

Not surprisingly, 90 percent of the respondents used performance information mainly to comply with government requirements. The next most significant use was to improve the design and quality of services (73 percent), followed by planning and budget allocation (71 percent). Less than 50 percent of respondents used performance information in policy development and advice.

Most respondents considered that performance information had helped to bring about many improvements. The greatest improvement identified was an employee focus on goals, either individual or organizational. Almost 70 percent of respondents identified better employee focus as a result of performance information, although it was less often important for improving motivation. This finding is consistent with the lack of alignment between organizational and individual performance goals already noted. Other significant effects were more manager accountability (61 percent), better service quality (62 percent), improvements in decisions (61 percent), and changes in budget allocations (57 percent). The changes in budget allocations were internal measures for reallocation within an appropriation rather than movement of resources between appropriations.

Less than 45 percent of respondents identified reduction in the cost of operations as a result. Performance information had little effect on the relationship with elected officials, which reinforces the finding that elected officials do not use performance information very intensively. Less than 5 percent of entities thought that performance information had negative effects.

Difficulties with the Performance System

Australia has been refining its national performance framework for more than 30 years. During that time there have been significant improvements in many aspects of the system, but there are also persistent challenges, many of which have existed since the arrangements were first introduced.

Political Support

The Australian Parliament has shown interest in getting better information on results since at least 1983, when a bipartisan parliamentary committee identified the need for public entities to give more attention to efficiency and cost effectiveness. That bipartisan commitment has been consistent throughout the last three decades. There has been considerable criticism of the quality and usefulness of performance information, but no dispute about the importance of the information itself.

Governments have taken different approaches to performance, and the connection between performance, results, and budgets has evolved. The main differences have been associated with political philosophy and the relationship desired between the elected and the administrative arms of government. For example, Labor governments have generally cultivated a collaborative relationship with career civil servants and have promoted performance information structures that emphasize the collection of data to inform policy and administration. Coalition governments, by contrast, have tended to reinforce the control and accountability attributes of performance arrangements. However, both sides of the political spectrum have been concerned about strengthening the transparency, quality, and relevance of performance information to its intended purposes. Despite the unanimous agreement on its importance, this has proved to be an endless challenge.

Capacity and Resources

One significant feature of the Australian public performance regime is that the center of government has invested relatively little in building effective performance structures across entities. Establishing and maintaining performance information has been seen as a normal running cost to be addressed within the global allocations for administration, with very little training and skills development by the center. Guidance and a short period of central training was provided after the Outcomes and Outputs arrangements were introduced but minimal new guidance and support was provided to line agencies to improve their quality and address situational challenges. There has also been little concern for quality assurance or ensuring that information is used effectively. The ANAO has commented on many occasions on the deficiency of support in its cross-agency audits of performance information (e.g., ANAO 2007, 2011).

In 2011 the Australian Parliament amended the Auditor-General Act 1997 to give the Auditor- General authority to audit the appropriateness of performance indicators and the completeness and accuracy of agency reporting. The ANAO is pilot-testing an approach to using this authority in three large entities before extending the practice across central government. This is expected to provide a solid basis for the ANAO examination of the quality of performance information. It will also give the ANAO an opportunity to make specific recommendations for improvement and better assure Parliament of the quality of the information it receives.

The DOF has responded to the calls for more substantial and coherent guidance on performance information requirements. In April 2015 it issued five new guidance documents to help entities to understand their PGPA Act obligations. It also provided guidance on how to develop relevant and useful performance information (DOF 2015a, 2015b, 2015c, 2015d, 2015e).

An interesting finding from the survey discussed is the significance of a performance culture in the Australian public sector. The main factor considered strongly or substantially important for most respondents was management and leadership, followed by organizational culture. In both survey responses and follow-up interviews respondents identified a high level of commitment to organizational goals as drivers of performance. Where performance was considered to have a significant impact, the existence of performance measures was closely associated with providing clarity of purpose and a focus for managers and staff.

The regional office of the DOF in Canberra (where most national government entities are based) established the Canberra Evaluation Forum soon after program evaluation became mandatory in the late 1980s. One illustration of the persistence of a performance culture is that the Forum still conducts regular meetings. The Institute for Public Administration, Australia also regularly conducts events based on performance themes and presents awards for the quality of annual reports that are highly prized by recipients. The Australasian Evaluation Society is also active in Canberra.

Data Trustworthiness

The ANAO plays a key role in monitoring the quality and usefulness of performance information. Since the mid-1990s it has completed many audits of various aspects of the performance framework and has consistently provided detailed recommendations and better practice advice to supplement information from government agencies. In its most recent report the ANAO identified as continuing major challenges to developing meaningful performance indicators (1) the limitations of a homogenous framework for a diverse range of functions and activities; (2) difficulties in providing coherent reporting on multi-agency activities; (3) bridging the gap between actions and outcomes can take several years to cause measurable change; (4) difficulties in measuring efficiency and clearly defined outcomes; and (5) the need for more rigorous independent assurance arrangements for entity performance reporting (ANAO 2013).

Conclusion

The Australian performance information system has evolved in many ways over a long period. At the beginning Australia sought to establish a system that identified fundamental connections between the resources allocated to entities and the results they achieved. This was later refined to focus on specific performance measures, with an emphasis on linking inputs to outputs and outcomes. Program evaluation was introduced to complement a shortage of information because performance indicators were flawed. Further attempts were made to improve the quality of performance indicators as the focus on centrally driven evaluation programs disappeared.

The DOF and in the last two decades the ANAO have been major drivers of organizational performance in the Australian public sector. The DOF was instrumental in the design and implementation of the FMIP, the centralized program evaluation initiative, the outcomes and outputs framework, and the drafting of the PGPA Act and associated regulations and guidance. The ANAO has been auditing performance-related matters since the early 1990s and has produced better-practice guides on a variety of performance-related topics. The Auditor General regularly makes speeches highlighting the importance of good performance information for transparency and accountability in public administration. There are also active discussion forums on performance matters in academia and professional organizations in Australia, although there is little published research on how performance is managed at any level of government.

Because the most recent changes to Australia's public performance regime are not yet fully in place, it is not possible to extract any lessons from practical experience with the changes. Instead, it is necessary to seek the lessons from the reasons for those changes and the differences that they are expected to make.

The main changes in performance arrangements since 2013 have been to give greater emphasis to entity-level planning and the integration of performance goals in mandatory corporate plans. These changes have been reinforced by a new format for reporting on progress toward those goals. The link between performance and budgets has been revised in order to reduce the amount of performance information in budget-related reports. Portfolio budget statements are being redesigned so that in future entities will only include "a strategically focused subset of performance information" (DOF 2015a) drawn from the detailed information in corporate plans. As a result, the locus of accountability for performance can be expected to move away from budget and appropriation documents to corporate plans and annual reports. The latter have traditionally received very little attention from Parliament, even though they are submitted within four months of the end of every financial year. If the new changes have any impact on the extent to which performance information helps to make operations and services in Australia more efficient or cost-effective, they could have significant implications for the practical relevance of performance budgeting not only in Australia but also in other countries. If not, Australia is likely to keep trying to refine its performance information arrangements rather than abandoning them.

Notes

1. For example, the Agriculture portfolio includes the Department of Agriculture, the Australian Grape and Wine Authority, the Fisheries Research and Development Corporation, the Rural Industries Research and Development Corporation, the Australian Fisheries Management Authority and the Australian Pesticides and the Veterinary Medicines Authorities, among others. A portfolio budget statement includes both an overview on matters covering the entire group and statements for each entity.

2. The *Public Governance, Performance and Accountability Act 2013* can be accessed at http://www.comlaw.gov.au/Series/C2013A00123.

3. The survey was undertaken by the author, with the endorsement of the Australian Department of Finance, as part of a postgraduate research program at the University of Canberra. The results have not previously been published. Information on the methodology, coverage and other matters relating to the work can be obtained from the author. The survey, methodology, and all documentation are the property of the author but the survey results presented in this paper may be quoted, subject to appropriate citation, with the author's permission.

Bibliography

Australian Government, Department of Finance and Deregulation. 2012. *Is Less More? Towards Better Commonwealth Performance.* Canberra: Commonwealth of Australia.

ANAO (Australian National Audit Office). 2004. *Better Practice in Annual Performance Reporting.* Canberra: Commonwealth of Australia.

———. 2007. *Application of the Outcomes and Outputs Framework.* Canberra: ANAO.

———. 2013. *Australian Government Performance Measurement and Reporting Framework, Pilot Project to Audit Key Performance Indicators.* Report 28, 2012–13. Canberra: ANAO.

———. 2014. *Pilot Project to Audit Key Performance Indicators.* Report 21, 2013–14. Canberra: ANAO.

Auditor-General. 2014. *Annual Report 2013–2014.* Canberra: Office of the Auditor-General.

Commonwealth of Australia. 2014. *Report of the Royal Commission into the Home Insulation Program.* Canberra: Commonwealth of Australia.

DOF (Department of Finance). 2015a. *Resources Management Guide no. 130: Overview of the Enhanced Commonwealth Performance Framework.* Canberra: DOF.

———. 2015b. *Resources Management Guide no. 131: Developing Good Performance Information.* Canberra: DOF.

———. 2015c. *Resources Management Guide no. 132: Corporate Plans for Commonwealth Entities.* Canberra: DOF.

———. 2015d. *Resources Management Guide no. 133: Corporate Plans for Commonwealth Companies.* Canberra: DOF.

———. 2015e. *Resources Management Guide no. 134: Annual Performance Statements for Commonwealth Entities.* Canberra: DOF.

———. 2015f. *Guide to Preparing 2015–16 Portfolio Budget Statements.* Canberra: DOF.

Hawke, Lewis. 2007. "Performance Budgeting in Australia." *OECD Journal on Budgeting* 7 (3). http://www.oecd.org/australia/43411866.pdf.

———. 2010. "Generating Quality Performance Information in Australia: Case Study 4.2." *Results, Performance Budgeting, and Trust in Government,* edited by Pedro Arizti, Jim Brumby, Nick Manning, Roby Senderowitsch, and Theo Thomas, 141–54. Washington, DC: World Bank.

———. 2012. "Australian Public Sector Performance Management: Success or Stagnation?" *International Journal of Productivity and Performance Management* 61 (3): 310–28.

———. 2013. *Survey of Performance Management in Australian Government Agencies.* Unpublished PhD material produced as part of the University of Canberra post-graduate research program.

Hawke, Lewis, and John Wanna. 2010. "Australia after Budgetary Reform: A Lapsed Pioneer or Decorative Architect?" In *The Reality of Budget Reform in OECD Nations,* edited by John Wanna, Lotte Jensen, and Jouke de Vries, 65–90. Cheltenham, United Kingdom: Edward Elgar.

Joint Committee of Public Accounts and Audit. 2013. *Review of the Auditor-General's Reports no. 11 to 31 (2012–13).* Canberra: Commonwealth of Australia.

Mackay, Keith. 2011. "The Performance Framework of the Australian Government, 1987 to 2011." *OECD Journal on Budgeting* 11 (3).

Murray, Andrew. 2008. *Review of Operation Sunlight: Overhauling Budgetary Transparency.* Canberra: Author.

OECD. 2008. *Performance Budgeting: A User's Guide.* OECD.

Parliament of Australia.1983. *Review of Commonwealth Administration.* Canberra: Author.

————. 1984. *Budget Reform: A Statement of the Government's Achievements and Intentions in Reforming Australian Government Financial Administration.* Canberra.

————. 1990. *Not Dollars Alone.* Report of the House of Representatives Standing Committee on Finance and Public Administration, Canberra.

————. 2007. *Transparency and Accountability of Commonwealth Public Funding and Expenditure.* Senate Finance and Public Administration Committee, Canberra.

CHAPTER 6

Estonia

Ringa Raudla

Introduction

The legal framework for incorporating performance data into budget documents has been in place in Estonia since the early 2000s. Despite the large volume of performance information that line ministries and their subordinate agencies provide during the budget process, actual use of performance data to inform budgetary decisions has been minimal.

Since the mid-2000s the Ministry of Finance (MoF) has adopted a variety of plans to tighten the links between performance information and budget decision-making. In March 2014 a new law allowed ministries to move from input-based categorization of budgeted expenditures to a program-based format in which expenditures would be categorized by performance areas, programs, and subprograms. Because it is too early to assess its effects, this chapter looks primarily at Estonia's experiences with performance budgeting over the past decade; it also discusses the reasons for the most recent reform.

The chapter draws on previous studies of performance budgeting and management in Estonia and on interviews with seven civil servants from the MoF, the Ministry of Education and Research, and the National Audit Office (NAO).

Performance Budgeting in Estonia

Requirements for Collecting and Disseminating Data

The current performance budgeting system was created between 2002 and 2005 via amendments to the organic budget law (the State Budget Act) and adoption of a regulation on strategic planning.[1] One motive for the reform was to modernize the budgeting system to demonstrate that Estonia is a developed country with advanced management practices. Proponents of the reform argued that adding performance information to budget documents would increase efficiency and transparency. The reform was influenced by the doctrine of New Public Management. It was also recommended by the International Monetary Fund (IMF) and the European Union (EU). (In the spring of 2014 the system was modified by a new organic budget law.) The new act allows, but does not require, ministries to move to program-based budgets.[2] Figure 6.1 shows the basic features of the performance budgeting system that has been in place for the last decade.

The first step in the annual budget cycle is preparation of the rolling State Budget Strategy (SBS), which the government adopts each year for the next four years.[3] Beforehand, the ministries must submit four-year financial and organizational development plans to the MoF.[4] The basic structure of the plans is established in the Strategic Planning Regulation and may be further elaborated by the MoF; in preparing its plan, each ministry has to consider all relevant strategic documents, among them the previous year's SBS, national and sectoral development plans (particularly areas of cooperation with other ministries), international obligations, the government's action program (i.e., the coalition agreement), and its own reports on progress to date on previous development and action plans. Development plans, which are usually organized by program and subprogram, specify (1) goals of the ministry and subordinate agencies for the next four years; (2) what will be done to achieve the goals; (3) expected outcomes and outputs; (4) indicators that reflect progress toward achieving the goals; and (5) performance targets. The associated financial plans specify the expenditures estimated for each policy area.[5]

Figure 6.1 Estonia: Strategic Planning and Performance Budgeting System

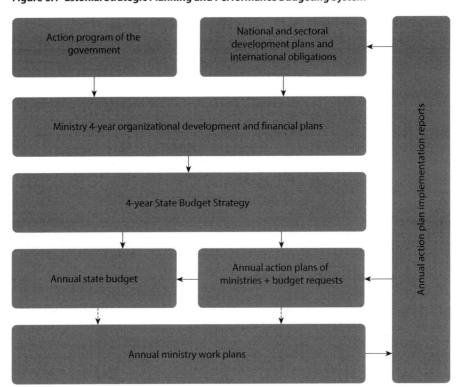

The MoF integrates ministry organizational development plans into the SBS. Thus, in addition to macroeconomic indicators and projected revenues and expenditures, the SBS contains a significant amount of performance information: it outlines the government's cross-cutting goals for the different policy fields and provides information about how progress toward the goals is measured and what the expected targets are for the next four years (see table 6.1 for an example for Estonia's education objectives). The SBS does not, however, break down expenditure projections by policy field ("performance area"). Expected spending for the next four years is classified by ministry.

After the SBS has been approved, the line ministries submit to the MoF annual operational ("action") plans and related budget proposals. These action plans, which are effectively one-year performance plans, outline, in more detail than the four-year plans, the ministry's goals, activities, performance targets, and indicators (current and expected levels). According to the Strategic Planning Regulation, ministry action plans are supposed to form the basis for budget negotiations and should contribute to the explanatory memorandum of the draft budget. As will be explained, in practice action plans are rarely discussed during budget negotiations. The expenditures in the budget plans submitted with the action plans are usually classified by policy area and category (e.g., operational expenditure, transfer, or investment). So far, however, expenditures in the draft budget law itself have only been classified according to the ministerial boundaries.

After the MoF and line ministries negotiate the budget, the cabinet approves the draft and submits it, together with supporting documents containing performance information,[6] to the parliament. Before adopting the budget law, the

Table 6.1 Education Performance Information, 2015–18 Estonian State Budget Strategy
percent

	Sector objective: The education provided in Estonia is of high quality, available, and responds to the needs of the learner and of society				
Indicator	Base target	Target 2015	Target 2016	Target 2017	Target 2018
Participation in preschool (4 years old to school age)	90.8 (2012)	95	95	95	95
Source: Eurostat **Responsible authorities:** Ministry of Education and Research (Ministry of Social Affairs, Ministry of Internal Affairs)	[95 (2012)]				
12–24-year-olds with little education not in further education or training	9.7 (2013)	11	11	10.5	<10
Source: Eurostat **Responsible authorities:** Ministry of Education and Research (Ministry of Justice, Ministry of Social Affairs, Ministry of Internal Affairs)	11.5 (2013)				
Proportion of teachers 30 and younger **Source:** Estonian Education Information System	10.3 (2013) [12.5 (2013)]	11	11.5	12	12.5

Source: SBS 2015–18.

Toward Next-Generation Performance Budgeting • http://dx.doi.org/10.1596/978-1-4648-0954-5

parliament discusses the budget in three plenary readings and can amend the draft budget, although there are some constitutional restrictions on the types of amendments that can be adopted (e.g., amendments have to be offsetting). The 11-member Finance Committee is one of the most important standing committees of the Estonian parliament and takes the lead in the budget deliberations, sometimes making recommendations about whether to incorporate proposed amendments into the budget.[7]

For day-to-day management, the ministries prepare work plans. Their structure and content are not centrally regulated, but usually the work plans describe in detail planned activities and deadlines. For some ministries there may be some overlap between the annual action plan (the performance plan) and the work plan, but usually work plans do not specify performance indicators.

Three months after the fiscal year ends, the ministries must submit to the MoF reports about how their annual operational plans were implemented.[8] The MoF issues guidelines for line ministries about how to complete these reports; current guidelines require a comparison of performance achieved against the targets (mostly quantitative) established in the annual action plans and explanations of why targets were or were not achieved. The MoF then consolidates the ministry reports into a single document, the state activity report, which is annexed to the consolidated annual report submitted to the legislature for approval. The Strategic Planning Regulation stipulates that the action plan reports should be taken into account when ministries draft the next four-year organizational development plans.

The four-year organizational development plans and the annual work plans are available to the public on individual ministry and agency websites but not on a central government website. Ministry action plans can also be found in the appendix of the explanatory note to the draft budget (the budget memorandum) submitted to the parliament, but the plans are not posted separately on individual ministry websites. Action plan reports are, however, included in the annual reports posted on ministry websites (together with the annual accounts) and the state's activity report can be accessed on the MoF website. All sectoral development plans are accessible at the central government website.[9]

In the 2014 budget law there is increased emphasis on cross-cutting goals and aligning performance targets in longer-term strategic documents with those in the operational plans. The overall MoF reform vision is to move from a system where organizational development plans are the main strategic planning instruments to one where sectoral development plans are the main instruments.[10] According to the reform plans, one ministry can have several sectors and more than one ministry can contribute to any single sector. The sectors, in turn, would be organized by program. In cases where several ministries contribute to a program, it will be divided into sub-programs (see the following section for more detail).

In sum, Estonia's current budgeting system can be thought of as *presentational* performance budgeting rather than full-fledged performance-*informed* budgeting (see table 6.2). Performance information is presented together with financial information and is in principle expected to be considered in appropriations discussions.

Table 6.2 Estonian Central Government Performance Systems

System	Characteristics

System established in 2002–05 (State Budget Act and Strategic Planning Regulation)	• Ministries must provide
	  – Four-year strategic plans,
	  – Annual performance plans, and
	  – Annual performance reports.

New State Budget Act adopted in 2014	• Ministries have the option to use program formats for classifying expenditures in the budget. • Cross-cutting goals are emphasized. • There is more emphasis on aligning goals and targets in strategic and performance plans. • The goal is to move to using only sectoral development plans instead of using organizational and sectoral development plans in parallel.

The new budget law does not mention performance budgeting, but provisions in the law and the Strategic Planning Regulation imply that the MoF and the line ministries should take performance information into account when preparing draft budgets. As discussed in the following section, however, linking performance information to budgetary decisions has been difficult; it is only occasionally discussed during negotiations and is rarely taken into account in appropriation decisions. The general goal of MoF reform efforts over the past decade has been to move toward performance-informed budgeting, but more recently there has been growing emphasis on program budgeting ("activity-based budgeting" in Estonia).

Links with Other Forms of Budgetary Analysis

Program Budgets

For the past decade, during the budget process ministries have been required to provide information about "policy fields" and "groups of activities" (which can be understood as programs) for achieving performance targets. Ministry organizational development plans are usually organized as programs that are aligned with the performance information they provide.[11] The current organizational development plan of the Ministry of Education and Research, for example, has been divided into six programs (groups of activities): education, research and development, youth, language, archives, and general administration. The Strategic Planning Regulation requires ministries to estimate how much programs outlined in their organizational development and annual operational plans would cost. In recognition of differences in the capacity of ministries to provide such information, this requirement has not been strictly enforced.[12] Still, some ministries have attempted to be more systematic in calculating the costs of programs, groups of activities, and individual activities.[13] However, the information on programs for the most part has not been linked to appropriations in the budget adopted by the legislature. In the planning and budgeting of EU structural funds and other foreign sources of financing, however, program-based budgeting predominates.[14]

As noted, the new budget law allows ministries to use program-based rather than the traditional input-based budget classification. According to the act, when a ministry uses a program-based format, expenditures are to be classified by performance area, program, and sub-program.

So far, how ministries divide their work into programs (or policy fields or areas of activity) has varied greatly. One aim of the new act is to establish a more uniform understanding of how ministry activities are divided into programs. Thus, the new law specifically defines what constitutes a program.[15] Where different ministries contribute to the same program, it would be divided into sub-programs so as to clarify what each ministry would contribute to the budget to achieve the program goals.

The MoF expects that more flexibility in using budgetary resources will make the program format more attractive to line ministries. Ministries can petition the MoF to adopt the program-based format; the MoF would then verify that the ministry's systems for strategic planning, activity-based costing, and accrual budgeting would be adequate to justify the switch. The MoF is currently drafting the format for the program-based approach.

Program Evaluation

The central government does evaluate programs, but there is no requirement that they be evaluated at regular intervals. The Supreme Audit Institution (the NAO) does conduct some performance audits, but usually only of programs that are problematic. There is no expectation that it regularly evaluate all programs. Thus, program evaluations are for the most part left to the ministries themselves, which vary considerably in the extent to which they undertake these. More systematic evaluations are required, however, for programs financed by EU structural funds. Programs are usually evaluated by outside contractors because ministries feel that they do not have sufficient internal capacity. They also feel that they do not have enough financial resources to commission all the program evaluations they would like (NAO 2012).[16] The ministries themselves link evaluation results to the performance information in development plans, action plan reports, or other documents, but there is no formal system governing such linkages.

Multiyear Budgeting Process

As noted, the core document in the Estonian budget process is the SBS, which covers four years and is compiled every year on a rolling basis. Currently, the SBS contains considerable performance information. Until 2014, it did not set binding ceilings on ministry spending,[17] but the new budget law requires the SBS to set ceilings for the next four years.[18] The SBS does not, however, estimate the cost of achieving particular goals or targets.

Changes in Performance Budgeting over Time

Because Estonia only regained its independence in 1991, it does not have much history of experimenting with administrative or public management reforms. In the 1990s reform efforts were directed mainly to creating democratic institutions and establishing a market economy. The goal of administrative reforms was to restructure the organizations inherited from soviet times and create a functioning civil service.

Before the current system of performance budgeting was created, starting in 2000 Estonia briefly experimented with a centrally mandated and government-wide pay-for-performance (PFP) scheme, but it was discontinued after a few years because it failed to achieve the intended goals (Nōmm and Randma-Liiv 2011). Critics said the reform was poorly planned and haphazardly implemented (Randma-Liiv 2005; see also NAO 2002). For example, subordinate agencies did not know in advance what the PFP criteria would be. Ministerial committees tasked with disbursing bonuses were often unwilling to differentiate between agencies: disbursements mostly reflected the number of employees an agency had. Within agencies, disbursements were also not systematic, and performance criteria and explanations for awards were rarely clear. In the end, the PFP was perceived to be an exercise that primarily increased the amount of paperwork without the supposedly performance-based-pay being connected to actual performance (Randma-Liiv 2005).

What lessons emerged from the brief PFP experiment? Among them were that:

1. The initiators of the reform had overrated the capacity and commitment of agency and ministerial leadership. The chaotic execution demonstrated the need for more extensive preparation and support (e.g., pilot projects, guidelines, and additional training).
2. The lack of commitment of senior managers made implementation even more difficult.
3. It became clear that adding PFP onto a system that produced only rudimentary performance data was unrealistic.
4. Finally, it was counter-productive to attempt reform when time pressures were acute. PFP proponents did not allow for the time it takes to carefully evaluate the experiences of other countries or to consider how to adapt PFP to the Estonian context (Randma-Liiv 2005). Since the centralized PFP system failed, it has been left to ministries to decide how to link pay to performance. Ministry practices vary a great deal.

Adoption of the Current System

Preparing the Ground, 2002–05
The basic features of the current performance budgeting system were put in place between 2002 and 2005 and updated in 2014. Although the new budget law lays a foundation for changing it, the basic features of the current performance management system can be expected to remain intact.

The MoF has been the lead designer of the current system, in coordination with the Estonian Government Office. Also, given Estonia's "new democracy" status, earning recognition from international organizations—having a good

international reputation—has been a major driver of its performance management initiatives (Nõmm and Randma-Liiv 2012). In creating the system, for
instance, the MoF consulted with the IMF. Drafting of the strategic planning
documents was also shaped by the EU accession process, EU membership, and
the receipt of structural funds.

The first step was to introduce the four-year strategy into the budget preparation process. Revisions to the State Budget Act in 2002 required ministries to
submit their goals and activities for the next four years to the MoF each spring.
In the same year, the organic budget law was amended to stipulate that preparation of the state budget must also take into account the goals of the ministries,
which were therefore required to submit annual operational plans with their
budget proposals.

The next major step in creation of a performance-oriented management system was made at the end of 2005 with the adoption of the Strategic Planning
Regulation, which stipulated the contents of various strategic documents and
also determined how the plans were to be used in the state budget process
(NAO 2012; Nõmm and Randma-Liiv 2011).

Moving beyond Presentational Performance Budgeting, 2006–14

By the mid-2000s Estonia had in place a system that could be categorized as
presentational performance budgeting, which brought significant amounts of
performance information into the budget process. The MoF was, however,
increasingly concerned about how rarely performance information was used in
making budgetary decisions (MoF 2007; NAO 2008). Since 2006 it has led a
process to help the central government move closer to performance-informed
budgeting (Raudla 2013). The IMF also suggested strengthening the measurement of performance and moving to program-oriented budget classification
(Kraan, Wehner, and Richter 2008). Preparation of the reform took eight years,
until the new law was adopted in 2014. The reform in many ways is still in process since many of the necessary regulations are yet to be drafted.

Preparation for the reform had three phases: (1) The concept paper of 2007;
(2) studies commissioned and pilot projects in 2008–12; and (3) drafting the new
budget law in 2013–14.

In 2007 the MoF drafted a concept paper on financial management reform
(MoF 2007) that envisioned both a move to program- and performance-based
budgeting and adoption of accrual budgeting. The concept paper was very ambitious; it proposed aligning annual budgets with the SBS,[19] reclassifying the budget itself on a program basis, and allocating funds for achievement of performance
goals rather than using input-based classification.[20] It was hoped that changing
the budget classification from a line-item to a performance-based format would
lead to more extensive use of performance information in making budget
decisions.

The concept paper raised the issue of whether organization of government
activities into programs or performance areas in the budget should follow
ministerial divisions or be horizontal, cutting across ministerial boundaries;

it recommended the former.[21] The concept paper also proposed adopting the SBS and ministry organizational development plans for four years after elections on a fixed rather than a rolling basis. The concept paper was submitted to the Cabinet in 2008. It was not approved. According to the NAO (2008), at this stage the Estonian central government was not yet ready to adopt such an extensive budgeting reform.

The MoF then sought to elaborate its approach, relying on a small three-person reform team, with a few assistants. Believing it lacked the time and capacity to complete the necessary analyses, between 2009 and 2012 the team sought advice from consultants; EU structural funds helped to cover the cost. Although outsourcing essential parts of the analytical preparation of the reform allowed the MoF to go beyond its in-house analytical capacities, it learned that such a strategy can give rise to significant problems:

- Since different parts of the reform were formulated by different consultants, the ultimate plan was fragmented and inconsistent. The fragmentation made it difficult for those involved to make fully informed contributions. Analysts involved in one phase of reform preparation did not know exactly what would be done in the next, so they found it difficult to understand how the particular policy they analyzed would fit with others.
- Contracting and managing the outside consultants not only had transaction costs, it also limited the time MoF staff had for substantive analysis.
- Finally, reliance on private consultants narrowed deliberations on the reform to their frameworks and was a barrier to analytical commentary or other participation by public sector organizations[22] (for a more detailed discussion of the outsourcing, see Raudla 2013).

The goal of the reform plans considered between 2008 and 2012 was to better link strategic planning and budgeting. Although the 2007 concept paper had envisioned a performance-based budget format that would follow ministerial boundaries, in the next few years reform ideas embraced a more cross-cutting approach: The budget would be organized in 5 strategic areas, 17 performance areas, and programs, which would all cut across ministerial boundaries. This vision, however, was overly ambitious, for which the MoF was increasingly criticized. Tension between strategic cross-cutting goals and the administrative realities of a system built around line ministries was inevitable. Although building bridges between ministerial silos was seen as a worthy goal, using the budget process to do so proved impossible. In addition, as the 2011 OECD report on public governance in Estonia emphasized, formulating strategic goals for the government should have also drawn upon politicians rather than being simply a "technocratic exercise."

By 2013 it had become clear that Estonia would have to move quickly to adopt a new budget law to fulfill the requirements of the EU Fiscal Compact.[23] Despite more than five years of preparation since 2007, there was still no clear blueprint for reform, and by 2013 the main members of the reform team had moved on from the MoF. Because there was not sufficient time to thoroughly discuss different options, the provisions of the new organic budget law concerning performance budgeting reflect pragmatic compromises and flexibility. For example, the new law allows the government to adopt a program-based budget format but does not mandate it, although the MoF does plan to move gradually to program classification of expenditures so that by 2021 all ministry budgets should be program-based. Such a gradual ministry-by-ministry approach reflects the fact that ministries are at different stages of preparedness in adopting systems for measuring performance and for activity-based costing. The MoF is also calling for replacement of organizational and sectoral development plans with sectoral development plans prepared according to the performance areas outlined in the SBS.[24] This could help reduce the administrative burden on ministries of preparing and reporting strategic plans.[25]

Use of Performance Information

Governmentwide Use of Performance Information

Although there are formal routines for ministries and agencies to consider performance data at least annually when putting together their four-year development plans, one-year action plans, and reports on how the action plans were conducted, they only occasionally use the information in making specific budgetary decisions (NAO 2008, 2012; OECD 2011, 2013; Raudla, Savi, and Liedemann 2013). Although line ministries submit significant amounts of performance information to the MoF during the budget preparation process and the data are discussed at least to some extent during budget negotiations (especially in discussions about the SBS), negotiation between line ministries and the MoF of specific appropriations do not usually focus on performance (NAO 2012; OECD 2011, 2013; Raudla, Savi, and Liedemann 2013). To a large extent, the budget process in Estonia is incremental, with the "base" not being subject to extensive analysis. Most budget negotiations deal with new ministry spending proposals, which do discuss performance data, but the concern of the MoF is to make sure that ministry budget requests remain within the MoF-imposed ceilings (NAO 2012).[26]

In preparing this report, MoF officials were asked about the reasons for limited use of performance information in making budget decisions. The following reasons were most prominent: (1) the MoF lacks the time or capacity to analyze the volume of information; (2) MoF officials simply do not know how to take performance information into account in making budget decisions; (3) the low quality of performance data sometimes renders the information unusable; (4) attribution problems (i.e., because the cause and effect links between spending and results are hard to demonstrate, it is not clear that failure to achieve certain indicators should result in changes to budgetary allocations); and (5) a large proportion of budgeted spending is mandated by law, regardless of performance (Raudla, Savi, and Liedemann 2013).

Line ministry officials had different explanations for the limited use of performance data. Some, for instance, believe that performance-based arguments would not convince the MoF. Ministries also do not have the capacity to analyze the links between resources, activities, outputs, and outcomes, making it harder to justify their arguments (NAO 2012). One ministry official stated that "If we tried to tell the Ministry of Finance in budget negotiations that specific activities and monetary contributions would influence the achievement of indicators, the ministry would not believe it, because the connection remains too abstract in the case of major indicators, which means that making budget decisions on this basis would be impossible" (NAO 2012, 24).

Internal uses of performance information for budgeting by line ministries tends to be guided by specific activities (the work plan) rather than performance documents (the development and action plans and the action plan report) or performance indicators (NAO 2012; Raudla, Savi, and Liedemann 2013). The barriers to use most often cited were familiar: many mandated expenditures,[27] attribution problems, lack of time and resources for analysis, and the political nature of budgetary decisions.[28] A structural barrier within line ministries is that the separate units responsible for budgeting and for strategic management "communicate infrequently and generally do not understand each other's work" (OECD 2011, 194).

Performance information is used even less in the parliamentary than in the executive phase of the budget process (Raudla 2012). To prepare themselves for committee meetings, some MPs on the finance committee do read the documents that contain performance data, but some never do.[29] Performance data are not discussed at all during finance committee meetings and do not shape committee decisions. Committee members identify multiple reasons for this: the documents are too long and cumbersome; the legislative budget process is too tightly scheduled to allow time to discuss performance data; and parliament has only a limited role in making substantive changes to the budget. Finance committee members also feel that the committee, which has only a small support staff, does not have the analytical resources to analyze the performance data that the executive branch submits (Raudla 2012).

Even if such information is not used extensively for making budget decisions, it is reasonable to ask whether the Estonian public sector uses it for managerial purposes. Here the evidence is mixed. On one hand, the NAO (2012, 3) concluded that in three of five ministries it audited, respondents were producing performance reports only because the MoF requires them but do not use them in making new choices. On the other hand, according to a survey of 300 senior Estonian central government officials by the EC's COCOPS project (Coordinating for Cohesion in the Public Sector of the Future), it appears that performance information is used for certain managerial purposes (Savi and Metsma 2013).

As figure 6.2 illustrates, more than half the respondents said that they apply performance indicators rather extensively to monitor the performance of their colleagues (72.8 percent), identify problems that need attention (71.9 percent), assess whether they reach their targets (71.8 percent), and foster learning and improvement (65.5 percent). In terms of external use, more than half the executives said they use indicators to manage the image of their organization (58.8 percent) and communicate to citizens and service users what their organization does

Figure 6.2 How Senior Estonian Officials Use Performance Information[a]

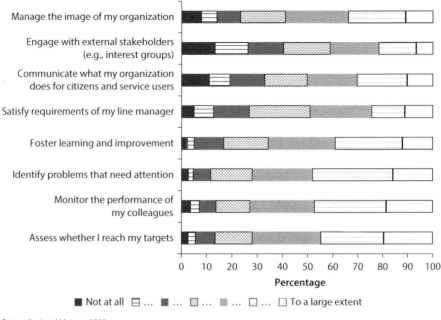

Source: Savi and Metsma 2013.
a. Responses to the survey question, "In my work, I use performance information to…"

(50.2 percent). There are somewhat contradictory perceptions in terms of using the indicators to engage with external stakeholders (e.g., interest groups): 40.2 percent assert they do not do so at all, but 41.2 percent claim to use them actively. The survey data also indicate that performance indicators are used less by ministerial officials than by officials in subordinate agencies (Savi and Metsma 2013).

Difficulties with the Performance System

Capacity and Resources

Insufficient analytical capacity has been a continuing major challenge for Estonian performance budgeting (Ministry of Finance of the Republic of Estonia 2007; NAO 2008, 2012; Nõmm and Randma-Liiv 2011; OECD 2011; Raudla, Savi, and Liedemann 2013). While ministry officials have had some training in strategic planning, performance measurement, and performance budgeting, they feel they need more resources to complete these processes successfully.[30] One consequence is that although significant amounts of performance data are indeed gathered, performance measures are often chosen based on what is already available (e.g., from the Statistical Office of Estonia or Eurostat). Furthermore, ministries feel that they lack the resources to interpret the data gathered, or to commission studies or program evaluations. This restricts their use of performance data in budget negotiations.

While more analytical capacity may be needed, performance budgeting processes already consume considerable resources. The current strategic planning and budgeting cycle in Estonia "is an onerous process that strains analytical capacity in the line ministries" (Kraan, Wehner, and Richter 2008, 19; see also NAO 2012). The ministries feel that most of their analytical energies go to fulfilling the requirements of the rather elaborate strategic planning system, which minimizes the time and resources left for analyzing the impacts of their activities (NAO 2012, 16). Recent MoF initiatives to reduce the number of strategic plans and duplicative reporting should help to reduce transaction costs.[31]

Too Much Data, Not Enough Information

Since performance budgeting began in the early 2000s, the volume of performance data generated by the Estonian central government has expanded significantly. Policymakers feel that despite all the data, however, there is not enough information that is useful in making better policy decisions. Performance indicators alone do not help to explain why certain targets were or were not reached and how to do better in the future. This is the result of the emphasis on planning and documentation and the relatively limited attention given to analysis (Kraan, Wehner, and Richter 2008).

Trust in Data and How It May Be Misused

Auditing performance data is left to the ministries and agencies themselves—the NAO is not mandated to conduct comprehensive audits of all the performance information they provide. If, in the course of a specific audit, questions arise about the quality of data (e.g., how it is gathered or interpreted), the auditors do investigate further and report on the problems. Policymakers generally see the performance information as reliable and indicative of actual performance (Raudla 2012). Cases of misrepresentation of data and some problems in how the data are interpreted[32] tend to be exceptions rather than the general pattern.

In putting together its report on the performance of the government as a whole, the MoF has tended to focus on successes and give little attention to unmet targets (NAO 2012, 28; see also NAO 2011). There has also been some tinkering with the targets, for example changing performance targets in the middle of the year to show up better in the yearend report (NAO 2012). Generally, however, ministries have few incentives to produce false data, manipulate performance data, or use data in a perverse way because there are no financial sanctions for not achieving the targets.

Political Support

Efforts to build up performance budgeting in Estonia attract only lukewarm, if any, attention from elected officials (Kraan, Wehner, and Richter 2008; OECD 2011; Raudla 2012, 2013). Reform efforts have had no political champion; instead, they have been led by the civil servants in the MoF. MoF officials have been criticized for not seeking sufficient input from elected officials into discussions of how to structure the performance budgeting system and for going ahead with reform preparations without political demand for it (NAO 2012; OECD 2011; Raudla 2012, 2013). Yet the elected officials themselves have not shown much interest in reform. During parliamentary discussions of the new budget law in the fall of 2013, the provisions pertaining to program budgeting, for example, received almost no attention, despite significant implications for the format of the annual budget. To expand the use of performance data in the budget process, the MoF needs extensive input from elected officials (see, e.g., OECD 2011). Otherwise, there is a danger that the budget process will be completely dominated by the executive, which could erode the parliament's democratic legitimization function when budget decisions are made.

From Measuring to Actually Using Data

While Estonian ministries are increasingly using performance information in making managerial decisions, such as for identifying problems and for learning, using it for making budget decisions is demonstrably rare (Ministry of Finance of the Republic of Estonia 2007; NAO 2012; OECD 2011; Raudla, Savi, and Liedemann 2013; Raudla 2012). Given the conceptual and analytical difficulties, further efforts to advance performance management in the Estonian central government could emphasize facilitating managerial use of data in ministries. Indeed, given the tight time schedule of the annual budget cycle, trying to subject performance data to the budget process has limited potential. Requiring ministries to hastily put together performance plans that the MoF has little time to analyze is not conducive to using performance data for improving learning and performance. How scarce analytical resources can best be used needs careful consideration. A top-down approach by the MoF that imposes routines for use of performance data may not be fruitful. Instead, ministries could be encouraged to create their own forums and routines for discussing performance information in terms of the needs of their specific policy responsibilities. Successful models could be shared with other ministries.

Broad Goals and General Change

In approaching performance budgeting, the MoF has given increasing attention to the cross-cutting goals of the government, consistent with the OECD (2011) review of Estonia. Although a number of steps have been taken to facilitate this horizontal perspective—e.g., structuring the SBS in terms of the cross-cutting goals, encouraging ministries to draw on them in formulating their organizational goals, choosing five priority areas on which ministries can base their sectoral development plans—there is still little inter-ministerial cooperation on strategic planning and performance budgeting. Moving to using sectoral (and by implication, inter-ministerial) development plans and program-based budgets that force ministries to share the budget of a program, as the MoF envisions, in principle represents a step forward in facilitating the whole-of-government approach, but whether that will actually happen remains to be seen. Such steps may instead be too radical a break with the way the Estonian central government is organized.

Furthermore, if poorly done that approach to strategic planning and budgeting may weaken lines of accountability in the public sector. It might be preferable to first pilot a cross-sectoral approach in a limited number of policy areas.

Conclusion

Performance budgeting in Estonia is in a state of transition. The system created in the first half of the 2000s led to a proliferation of performance plans and indicators that were of little use when budget decisions were actually made. Estonian ministries have become better technically at goal-setting, selecting performance indicators, and setting targets. However, the profusion of data has not necessarily provided actionable information. So much of the analytical capacities of the ministries has been consumed in complying with requirements to produce strategic plans and reports that little has been left for analysis.

Over time, the MoF has become significantly more realistic about the scope of reform. The highly ambitious performance-budgeting concept formulated in 2007 would have led to a radical change in the budget process. Reformers have become more aware of limitations in Estonia, such as scarce analytical resources and considerable variation in the capacities of different ministries to collect and use performance data. Thus the current incremental approach is certainly more realistic than more dramatic reform would be. For example, allowing the ministries themselves to choose whether and how fast they adopt program budgeting is a pragmatic recognition of the variations in ministerial analytical systems. Whether the ministries will actually take this opportunity and whether the program classification will improve budgetary decision-making is not yet clear.

Given the complexities of using performance data for making budget decisions, however, future reform efforts should be directed at thinking about how to encourage use of the information for other managerial purposes. It has been found that managers in ministries and agencies are the most likely users of performance data, because they find it useful for identifying problems, organizational learning, and designing corrective measures. If production of performance data were not subject to the tight time schedule and analytical formats prescribed by the budget process, officials in line ministries might have more opportunities to generate information that would better serve their own organizational needs.

Notes

1. Government of the Republic, Regulation on "Types of Strategic Development Plans and Procedure for Preparation, Amendment, Implementation, Evaluation of and Reporting on Strategic Development Plans" was adopted on December 13, 2005.

2. The English version of the law, the State Budget Act, is available at: https://www.riigiteataja.ee/en/eli/504072014004/consolide.

3. Estonia's state budget strategies are available in English at http://www.fin.ee/budgeting.

4. The organizational development plans that ministries submit also cover their subordinate agencies.

5. The level of detail about projected expenditures for different policy areas varies considerably by ministry.

6. The MoF usually consolidates the annual action plans of the ministries into a single appendix to the explanatory note of the draft budget. The explanatory note itself may also include the most important performance information.

7. Amendments during the legislative phase usually cover only about 0.2 percent of expenditures (Kraan, Wehner, and Richter 2008, 23).

8. In addition to the annual action plans, ministries are expected to prepare annual reports on the progress of the sectoral development plans. These reports, however, are not directly linked to the organizational development plans or reports. Furthermore, as noted by the OECD (2011), in reality reports are provided for only about one-third of the sectoral development plans.

9. https://valitsus.ee/et/eesmargid-tegevused/arengukavad.

10. The SBS currently outlines 23 "performance areas"; the vision of the MoF is that in future, ministries will submit sectoral development plans only for these performance areas, rather than submitting both sectoral development and organizational development plans.

11. The level of detail in organizing activities as programs, however, varies significantly. While some ministries distinguish between very broad policy fields, others have more detailed classifications of activities. Also, over time the organization of' activities into programs has varied within the ministries themselves (NAO 2008). For example, in 2006, the Ministry of Education and Research divided its activities into 6 policy fields, in 2007 into 1, and in 2008 into 6. With regard to "measures" (groups of activities), the numbers were 21 in 2006, 23 in 2007, and 27 in 2008.

12. Given the significant uncertainty then surrounding budget revenues and expenditures, during the crisis of 2008–10 ministries were not required to provide this information.

13. Again, the degree of detail at which they do it varies significantly by ministry.

14. The English version of the 2007–13 Structural Assistance Act, which governs the use of EU funds, is accessible at https://www.riigiteataja.ee/en/eli/510072014012/consolide.

15. "The program is a development document which determines the measures, indicators, activities and financing scheme targeted at the achievement of a sub-objective of a policy area." (§ 19 s. 5) The act also stipulates that "The program shall be prepared in compliance with the budget strategy period. The program shall be approved by the minister."

16. The Ministry of Education and Research, for example, allocates about €100,000 euros a year for purchasing analyses and evaluations (NAO 2012).

17. Expenditure projections for ministries (and their governing areas) were called for in the state budget strategies in 2006 and 2007 but they were regarded as indicative rather than binding. During and after the crisis (2008–12), the SBS did not provide a format for ministry expenditure projections.

18. The budget law permits these ceilings to be adjusted in following years "only in case the general objective of a performance area, the action program of the Government of the Republic, the main directions of the state fiscal policy, the macroeconomic forecast, financial forecast, or legislation have materially changed" (art 22.2).

19. It was proposed that SBS objectives and targets would be established for four years and the budget law itself would set the annual objectives, targets, and outputs.

20. According to the concept paper, it was hoped that reform would make the use of resources more efficient, allow for better prioritization, and raise the quality of public services (Ministry of Finance of the Republic of Estonia 2007).

21. It was argued that this would make the reform more feasible and also help to clarify lines of responsibility for the ministries (Ministry of Finance of the Republic of Estonia 2007). The concept paper added, however, that if ministries increased their analytical capacities in the future, movement to cross-cutting classification could be considered.

22. In assessing the MoF reform preparation efforts, the NAO (2012, p. 30) concluded that "the activities of the Ministry of Finance in the development of financial management have been aimless and poorly organized."

23. The Fiscal Compact—the Treaty on Stability, Coordination and Governance in the Economic and Monetary Union—required Eurozone members, inter alia, to establish a structural budget balance rule and an independent fiscal council.

24. Ministries can still use organizational development plans if they do not have sectoral development plans that would cover their activities comprehensively.

25. So far, ministries have had to provide implementation plans and reports about both sectoral and organizational development plans.

26. Although MoF officials are expected to analyze the performance information that line ministries submit, these analyses are usually limiting to ensuring that the performance documents comply with the formal requirements – whether the goals are clearly worded, performance indicators measurable, and activities-outputs-outcomes logically connected – rather than discussing what the performance information implies for resource allocation decisions (NAO 2012).

27. According to NAO, about 75% of budgeted expenditures in the budget are fixed by laws, external obligations, of external support (NAO 2012, p. 23).

28. There are some exceptions to that general trend. For instance, in the Ministry of Interior homeland security area expected outputs have sometimes been used in making allocation decisions; and in the Ministry of Social Affairs spending on non-mandated programs is reviewed and if the programs are not deemed to be effective, their funding is discontinued (NAO 2012; Raudla, Savi, and Liedemann 2013).

29. Based on interviews with the members of the finance committee.

30. For example, in the Ministry of Economic Affairs and Communication, there are only two or three people to carry out the main analyses in all policy areas. and the total annual budget for contracting analyses is about €200,000 (NAO 2012).

31. For example, during the second half of the 2000s, the number of strategic plans ballooned to 200 (OECD 2011), but by a conscious MOF effort, the number has been reduced to about 30-40 strategies.

32. For example, in one case the authority in charge of providing financial support to enterprises used flawed methodology in measuring their performance in terms of jobs created to bulk up the performance indicators.

Bibliography

Jõgiste, Kadri, Peeter Peda, and Giuseppe Grossi. 2012. "Budgeting in a Time of Austerity: The Case of the Estonian Central Government." *Public Administration and Development* 32: 181–95.

Kraan, Dirk-Jan, Joachim Wehner, and Kirsten Richter. 2008. "Budgeting in Estonia." *OECD Journal on Budgeting* 8 (2): 1–40.

Ministry of Finance of the Republic of Estonia. 2007. "Riigi finantsjuhtimise arendamise kontseptsioon" ["The Concept Paper for Developing Public Financial Management"]. Ministry of Finance of the Republic of Estonia.

NAO (National Audit Office of Estonia). 2002. *Tulemusjuhtimiseks eraldatud töötasuvahendite kasutamine* [*The Use of Pay-for-Performance Funds*]. Audit Report. Summary in English available at www.riigikontroll.ee.

———. 2008. *Rahandusministeeriumi tegevus eelarvestamise põhimõtete kujundamisel* [*Activities of the Ministry of Finance in Developing Budgeting Principles*]. Audit Report. Summary available in English at www.riigikontroll.ee.

———. 2009. *Riigikutseõppeasutuste ümberkorraldamise tulemuslikkus.* [*Effectiveness of the Reorganization of Public Vocational Educational Institutions*]. Audit Report. Summary in English available at www.riigikontroll.ee.

———. 2011. *Overview of the Use and Preservation of State Assets in 2010.* Annual report by the National Audit Office to the Parliament.

———. 2012. *Activities of Government of the Republic in Assessing Impact of its Work and Performance Reporting.* Audit report. http://www.riigikontroll.ee/tabid/206/Audit/2265/Area/1/language/et-EE/Default.aspx.

Nõmm, Külli, and Tiina Randma-Liiv. 2012. "Performance Measurement and Performance Information in New Democracies." *Public Management Review* 14 (7): 859–79.

OECD (Organisation for Economic Co-operation and Development). 2011. *Estonia: Towards a Single Government Approach.* OECD Public Governance Reviews, OECD Publishing. https://riigikantselei.ee/sites/default/files/content-editors/Failid/oecd_public_governance_review_estonia_full_report.pdf.

———. 2013. "Government at a Glance 2013." http://www.oecd-ilibrary.org/sites/gov_glance-2013-en/04/04/index.html;jsessionid=268hevcjr0vnf.x-oecd-live-01?contentType=&itemId=%2Fcontent%2Fchapter%2Fgov_glance-2013-29-en&mimeType=text%2Fhtml&containerItemId=%2Fcontent%2Fserial%2F22214399&accessItemIds=%2Fcontent%2Fbook%2Fgov_glance-2013-en.

Randma-Liiv, Tiina. 2005. "Performance Management in Transitional Administration: Introduction of Pay-for-Performance in the Estonian Civil Service." *Journal of Comparative Policy Analysis: Research and Practice* 7 (1): 95–115.

Raudla, Ringa. 2012. "The Use of Performance Information in Budgetary Decision-Making by Legislators: Is Estonia Any Different?" *Public Administration* 90 (4): 1000–15.

———. 2013. "Pitfalls of Contracting for Policy Advice: Preparing Performance Budgeting Reform in Estonia." *Governance: An International Journal of Policy, Administration, and Institutions* 26 (4): 605–29.

Raudla, Ringa, Riin Savi, and Ermo Liedemann. 2013. "The Use of Performance Information in Cutback Budgeting: The Case of Estonia." Paper presented at the EGPA Annual conference in Edinburgh, United Kingdom, September 11–13.

Savi, R., and M. Metsma. 2013. *Public Sector Reform in Estonia: Views and Experiences from Senior Executives.* Country Report as part of the COCOPS Research Project. http://www.cocops.eu/wp-content/uploads/2013/06/Estonia_WP3-Country-Report.pdf.

CHAPTER 7

France

Frank Mordacq

Introduction

Parliament's unanimous vote on the LOLF (*loi organique relative aux lois de finances*: Organic Financial Law), a constitutional bylaw passed in 2001, launched performance budgeting in France. It radically changed the budgetary and accounting rules; starting in 2006 France moved from line-item to program budgeting and from cash to accrual accounting.

The program budget is structured based on major political objectives. France has broken with the tradition of expenditure-oriented budgets by drawing up a program budget with a three-tier structure, in which missions correspond to the state's public policy priorities. Some missions are "multi-ministry," pulling together all the programs, such as research, conducted by different ministries that relate to the same general policy. Each mission comprises programs to which appropriations are allocated, broken down by subprograms, the actions that together constitute the operational resources with which a program will be implemented. The previous structure based on "budget chapters" (line items) obscured the aims of budget appropriations and the cost of administrative policies and structures. By structuring the budget in terms of public policy objectives, the state's missions and public service goals become fully transparent.

Allocations were consolidated to allow more flexible management. Previously, ministers and the services they manage received appropriations through a large number of separate budgets, one for each self contained chapter. Since passage of the LOLF, appropriations may be freely apportioned among programs; allocations by subprogram and type of expenditure are now purely indicative. This arrangement allows for much more flexible management because those in charge of individual programs can reallocate appropriations as needed. Because of its very long-term effect on public finances, personnel expenditure is the only exception to the consolidation principle; it cannot be topped up with other appropriations and numbers of personnel and payrolls are capped.

Formerly, certain departments tried to use up their entire annual appropriation with a view to obtaining the same amount the following year; the appropriation carryover regime has now been relaxed to encourage management of multiyear appropriations: carryover of up to 3 percent of any appropriation can be negotiated, and each year ministers have multiyear commitment authority in addition to their appropriations for that year.

The system operates on a commitment accounting basis, which means that legal commitments, such as procurement contracts, international commitments, and multiyear subsidies, are registered in the data system; this makes multiyear program management more transparent because the amount of cash necessary to fulfill each year's legal commitments is specified.

Line ministries have more autonomy, and more accountability. With the LOLF system, each program, whether national or local, has a clearly identified program manager. Thus the French government is setting up a chain of responsibilities.

At the local level, each national program is given a program operating budget (BOP), which is a management budget envelope. Spending departments, which are allocated a budget total structured along the lines of the national program budget, have considerable latitude to allocate appropriations according to their assigned goals, with leeway to make allowances for local specifics. Local departments thus have a substantive part in managing state policies, though they must do so in conformity with a centrally defined strategy. This new relationship between central and decentralized departments calls for goal-oriented management and dialogue.

With the LOLF, a new public accounting system became necessary. Previously, in essence public accounting tracked execution of spending and revenue on a cash basis. To align itself with budgetary reform, the French state has set up an accounting system that incorporates cash-basis methods in the accrual accounting model as practiced by business and management for purposes of analyzing program costs. With the new budget and accounting classification, the French administration has been able to measure the cost of its public policies and value its asset base (land, property, debts, etc.). Finally, government accounts are certified by the State Audit Office (*Cour des comptes*).

Performance Budgeting in France

The LOLF (article 7-1) states that "A program covers appropriations for implementing an action or a consistent set of actions coming under the same ministry and involving both specific objectives defined in the public interest and expected results subject to review."

Managers must commit to performance goals. In exchange for their high degree of autonomy, managers must be fully committed to the goals of their programs and be accountable for progress toward results indicators and target values. Performance is measured by three criteria: social and economic effectiveness (outcomes), quality of service, and efficiency. The criteria thus reflect the standpoints of citizens, users, and taxpayers. Every year, ministers and program managers commit to achieving specific results through an annual performance plan (APP), which is appended to the Budget Act along with the program appropriations requests, the main goals relating to each program, performance indicators, and expected results. Combining into one document financial data and measurements of its performance makes it easier to assess the performance and efficiency of public policy.

Managers are held accountable for program performance. In the former system, there was not enough focus on the effectiveness of public spending; instead the emphasis was on complying with spending authorizations. The newer program-oriented budgets mean that spending departments are accountable to Parliament for their management decisions, their actual expenditures, their management of human resources, and the quality of what they accomplish in terms of the resources they have been allocated. When the budget has been executed, explanations of these points are included in an annual performance report (APR) appended to the Budget Review Act. The APR tracks the APP to make it easier to compare authorizations with execution. Finally, the APR for the past year must be submitted to Parliament and reviewed before the current year's Budget Act is passed. This requirement that execution of the previous budget must be reported before the next budget can be debated constitutes what is known as the "virtuous chain."

To reach political consensus on what constitutes performance, the Central Budget Authority (*Direction du budget*, here CBA) has written a methodological guide that has been signed off on by the Ministry of Finance (MoF), the chairman of the financial committee and the general rapporteur of the budget of each Assembly, the chairman of the State Audit Office, and the president of the interministerial committee of program audit (CIAP question 2-2; *Guide Général D'audit Des Programmes, Septembre* 2009).

APPs and reports have the same general structure and provide very rich information. In the APP, each mission has one document consisting of several programs: each document sets out strategy of the mission, medium-term expenditure framework (three years), appropriations sought in the budget bill, main objectives, and indicators.

Within the mission each program sets out the following:

- A strategic presentation of program
- Names of the minister and program manager accountable
- Objectives and indicators by classification (effectiveness, quality, efficiency)
- Comments and data sources (with results of prior years and targets for coming years)
- A detailed presentation of appropriations (with a summary of prior years) as a matrix both with an indicative action-based presentation ("destination") and indicative expenditure-class based presentation ("classification by nature": personnel, operating expenditure, capital expenditure, subsidies)
- Description of tax exemptions related to the program (named "tax expenditures")
- First-euro justification (explanation of all the main expenditures with activities indicators)

- List and details of categories of jobs financed by the program
- Description of the main agencies (*operateurs*) financed by program subsidies or tax revenues
- An itemization of program and agency jobs; cost analysis (support functions distributed in operational programs).

Creating and Disseminating Data

According to the LOLF, the Minister of Finance, in the name of the Prime Minister, presents the budget bill and is responsible for executing the Budget Act. Because the budget documents present goals and indicators for each program (the APP is appended to the budget bill), the CBA is responsible for performance. The CBA must check whether the proposals of goals and indicators that line ministries present adhere to the methodological guide for performance. For instance, it can reject goals and question the rationale for target indicators.

But the debate does not focus enough on results. The discussions between the CBA and line ministries take place in performance conferences, which discuss the choice of indicators and targets and are separate from the budget conferences in which appropriations are negotiated. The State Audit Office does not believe the performance conferences are concerned enough with reviewing performance.

The CBA is much more interested in efficiency objectives than in outcomes or quality. Between 2006 and 2015, the percentage of the indicators that relate to efficiency went up from 25 to 34 percent.

In an agreement between the executive and the legislative branches, France has decided to use performance data both for communicating through the documents given to Parliament and for management control of program administration. The consequence is a huge number of program goals and indicators. In 2006, the first year the LOLF went into effect, the APR specified 650 goals and 1,300 indicators for the 130 programs of the general budget. By 2015, these were down to 331 goals and 677 indicators for 120 programs. In recent years, efforts have been made to improve and simplify the presentation and to make it easier for parliamentarians to understand:

1. The strategic goals of the mission and the relevance of the associated indicators have been clarified, as was recommended by the State Audit Office (its report on the state budget in 2013 said that mission indicators did not always permit "parliamentarians to identify mission priorities and thus feed the political debate"). Indeed, these indicators, selected from existing program indicators, did not always inform public policy as a whole. In the 2015 performance plans, there were 98 state budget mission indicators, 14 of which were not directly from programs.
2. "Mission indicators" were examined in terms of three criteria: relevance to the strategic objectives; how representative they were of the mission's budgetary

importance; and whether they could be benchmarked to indicators used internationally. To meet these criteria, ad hoc indicators were added to be more representative of the whole of the mission. For example, the mission "Economy" in 2015 had a new indicator, the "ranking position of France in *Doing Business*," a report published annually by the World Bank, to account for the objective "to develop the legal and administrative environment for the creation and growth of business."

3. Program objectives were clarified and performance indicators were limited to those that were "relevant," "auditable," and "useful." Indicators must be used to improve service to the citizen or to reduce costs. The Budget Directorate and line ministries have sought to suppress activity indicators, means of compliance, and pilots of assistance services, which still turn up in performance plans. Some were offered in support of performance analysis (justification targets and trajectories) or in "the first euro justification" (which means explanation of appropriations). Also deleted were indicators that do not correspond to identified objectives, are not representative of the main state priorities and appropriations, or where the results were only slightly different (same targets met and a flat trajectory).

Table 7.1 shows use of data by the LOLF in terms of different components of performance budgeting in the general budget.

According to the OECD typology of performance budgeting,[1] France is a country in which performance informs budgeting. The one clear exception is universities, where funding is much more directly linked to results.

Table 7.1 Evolution of the Performance Indicators Used in Budget Programs

Category of indicator	2007	2010	2015
Effectiveness (for citizens)	51%	48%	46%
Quality (for users)	22%	19%	20%
Efficiency (for taxpayers)	27%	33%	34%

Data	2007	2010	2015
Number of missions	34	33	31
Number of programs	131	130	120
Number of objectives	569	442	331
Objectives per program	4.3	3.4	2.8
Number of indicators	1,173	925	677
Indicators per objective	2.1	2.1	2
Indicators modified	260	118	158
Modified indicators (%)	22%	13%	23%
New indicators (no.)	159	104	41
New indicators (%)	14%	11%	6%
Nonmodified indicators (%)	64%	76%	71%

Toward Next-Generation Performance Budgeting · http://dx.doi.org/10.1596/978-1-4648-0954-5

Accountability

For each program, the minister appoints a manager. Program managers are the linchpin of the new public management system, operating at the nexus between political and management accountability. Reporting to the minister, they help define the strategic objectives for their programs. They are the guarantors that operational plans will go into effect and commit to the achievement of the associated goals.

The APPs express the commitments of the program managers, presenting the strategies and objectives of each program and justifying to Parliament program appropriations and job requests. Program managers organize management control, in conjunction with those responsible for the BOPs. In return, they are allocated an overall amount to control. This gives them a great deal of freedom to choose where and how to allocate the financial and human resources they have available to meet their objectives. Their choices and the effects are reported in the APRs.

In the general state budget there are about 80 program managers, who are secretaries general or central administration directors. Of these 60 percent are responsible for a single program, the others for two or three. For example, for the interministerial mission National Education (*Enseignement Scolaire*), there are six programs, five being the responsibility of the Minister of National Education, and one the responsibility of the Minister of Agriculture. They are managed as follows:

- National primary education: Director General for National Education
- National secondary education: Director General for National Education
- Student life at school (*vie de l'élève*): Director General for National Education
- Private education: Director for Financial Affairs
- National education support functions: Secretary General for the Ministry of Education
- Agricultural Technical Education: Director General for Agricultural Education and Research

Regarding dialogue management, the new public management methods introduced by the LOLF are deployed in the BOPs in a bottom-up approach to users, the general public, and local authorities to improve public policy effectiveness. The BOP replicates part of a national program to cover a given scope of activities or geographic area. This means it takes up elements presented in the APPs (activities, performance, and budget) and applies them to a specific operational context. BOP managers and their operational units are thus responsible for proposing, programming, and implementing the program activities best suited to their specific environment.

With the BOPs public finance managers on the ground prepare and manage a local budget with an overall control total. For most the level of operating budgets is the region (22 plus 4 overseas) and sometimes the "inter-region" (supra-level).

Each government service customizes the national objectives as appropriate to guarantee optimal public action and rally staff to the performance-based approach. At the local level program performance indicators in the BOPs are tailored to specific local needs and circumstances, including a wide range of unemployment rates, industrial risks, crime rates, youth employment situations, etc. Program performance indicators may be:

- replicated directly, if possible, and broken down into targets suitable for regions or activities;
- translated into interim indicators if necessary: activity objectives, outputs, process objectives, modalities of action, measures to improve organization, management; or
- rounded out as needed by additional locally specific indicators, provided they do not contradict those in the APP.

Link to Other Forms of Budget Analysis

As far as internal budget analysis is concerned, inspection entities evaluate or audit ministries and cross-cutting public policies. Their audits are independent and their reports are given to the ministers and, with some exceptions, not published.

Over the last 10 years, both right- and left-wing governments have authorized many audits of public policies and program reviews, such as modernization audits (2005–07); general reviews of public policies (2007–12); and public action modernization (starting in 2012). All have been conducted by inspections units, mainly under the direction of the traditionally powerful *inspection des finances* with the assistance of private consulting firms. Some audits have been published on the MoF website.

The French constitution, amended in 2008, says (sections 24 and 47-2) that Parliament is responsible for evaluating public policies with the assistance of the State Audit Office. The State Audit Office presents a yearly budget execution report on both the use of appropriations and the results of programs. Comprehensive audits are also done on some public policies, financed by different public institutions, such as central government, agencies, or local authorities.

The commissions of each Assembly of Parliament present reports for each mission (made up of several programs) both for the budget bill and for the Budget Review Act. In this case public hearings sometimes give members of Parliament the opportunity to question ministries on results, but in practice, MPs and line ministries are not deeply interested in performance and the media do not report on it.

According to the constitution (section 47-2), each year financial committees of Parliament may ask the State Audit Office for reports of evaluations of public policies (there are usually six to eight each year).

In 2002 the government set up the Inter-ministerial Program Audit Committee (CIAP) to pool the expertise of ministry general inspectorates. This in-house audit structure has two assignments: help find the best way for each program to implement the LOLF principles, and guarantee the relevance and reliability of information attached to budget bills to ensure that Parliament can hold informed debates and votes.

CIAP is tasked with assessing the reliability of the results reported in APRs and the objectivity and comprehensiveness of the rationale given to justify deviations from stated APP targets. CIAP has one representative from each ministry inspection or audit body and is chaired by a general inspector of finance. Once a year, in association with the State Audit Office, it circulates a list of programs to be audited. Each audit is conducted by a team of three, one of whom is a member of the ministry whose program is audited. Each audit culminates in a report that presents observations and makes recommendations to the ministry concerned to improve the quality of the information it produces.

The ministry audited is invited to respond to the content of the audit report and especially to give its opinion on the proposals it makes. CIAP then issues an opinion that is based on the audit report and the ministry's response. Because CIAP's work is intended for ministry inspection bodies, its reports are not published. However, pursuant to their right to be kept informed, Parliament and the State Audit Office receive CIAP audit reports and opinions.

In 2012, six years after the LOLF went into effect, the main role of CIAP was reconsidered and some of its responsibilities were assumed by the new Internal Audit Harmonization Committee, which sets good practices for internal audits in line ministries.

Changes in Performance Budgeting over Time

Previous Performance Systems

The first experiences of performance budgeting were in the 1970s when the French administration applied the U.S. Planning, Programming and Budgeting System (PPBS), the *Rationalisation des choix budgétaires* (RCB), mainly to the Ministry of Defense. This experience failed, mainly because it was too theoretical and was disconnected from budget authorizations.

Starting in 1990, a new process described by Prime Minister Michel Rocard as "renewal of public service" was put in place based on globalization, "contractualization," responsibility, and evaluation. The Anglo-Saxon New Public Management theory had produced examples of new methods. During the1990s the French Department of Budget experimented with globalization of the current expenditures of the Ministry of Interior, signed agreements with the Tax Directorate and some other agencies on the level of appropriations for three years (with a guarantee that they could be carried over), the number of jobs (with a productivity rate), and also performance targets. Moreover, documents were prepared on how line ministries were to present budget appropriations by programs of public policies (*agrégats*), setting out objectives and indicators of performance. These experiences were very useful in 2001 when the Budget Department and the Parliament were negotiating the LOLF. These lessons emerged from this process:

1. Documents on performance that are not linked with the budget process or are not official are not helpful. Line ministries do not take them seriously and the MoF cannot manage them to meet its needs.
2. Analysis is not the right approach. Building programs based on all the appropriations related to a single public policy is not manageable. The budget bill is political; it is an authorization of specialized appropriations so that the administration can conduct public policy. It does not constitute an analysis of the full cost of public policies. Program managers have to manage their own appropriations and the jobs for which they are accountable. This was one reason that PPBS and RCB failed in France.
3. The Budget Department needs to build the skills of a dedicated team in charge of performance. Here, a consensus on the meaning and use of performance is essential. That is the reason why France was inspired by how the UK was using performance information in budget decision making.

Adoption of the Current System

The decision to adopt performance budgeting was made in 2001 with the vote authorizing the LOLF. Based on its previous experiences the Budget Department inserted a performance requirement in the organic law in order to secure the full agreement of Parliament.

It took another four years to design the new budget system (2002–06), and a new Budgetary Reform Directorate was put in place next to the Budget Directorate to support this process. Alain Lambert, the minister appointed in 2003—who as senator had proposed the organic law—was given the title Minister of Budget and Budgetary Reform. The Department of Finance (or Budget) took the lead in implementing program budgeting with the full support of the Prime Minister. According to the rules promulgated by the Budgetary Reform Directorate, each line ministry presented its proposals for missions, programs, objectives, and indicators. Where there were disagreements about the choice of missions and programs, these were decided by the Prime Minister. The French Parliament was also closely involved in the preparation, giving advice and asking the government to report annually on its progress toward implementing the reforms

Since 2006 a National Assembly multiparty information commission (MILOLF, *Mission d'Information Relative à La Mise En Œuvre De La Loi Organique Relative Aux Lois De Finances*) has reported every year or two on how the LOLF is working. In 2011 the State Audit Office presented a report of the first 10 years of LOLF. In 2014, the effect of accrual accounting was evaluated.

Use of Performance Information

The French Parliament is not involved enough in evaluation of results. In an LOLF report of the National Assembly in 2011, the deputies wrote, "We have failed to meet the budget review act deadline."

Under the review act, APRs are given to Parliament five months after the end of the fiscal year, and hearings of line ministries are organized by each commission for public discussion, but these sessions are more focused on appropriations and politics than performance results. Nevertheless, some public policies are evaluated in depth during these sessions depending on the work program of each commission. But there is no systematic rolling schedule for regularly evaluating each budget program, say every three or five years.

The government uses performance data in the annual budget negotiations to inform budgeting, but not to drive decisions. The main exception is allocations for universities. In 2007, during the Sarkozy presidency, agencies like universities, which were formerly financed from the central government budget, were given autonomy for budgets, human resources management, and assets management. Their management has since had room to maneuver—but they also have to enhance their performance.

About 20 percent of the appropriations for universities are based on their results in education (student attendance, success rate for award of degrees, position in the Shanghai ranking of world universities) and in research (publications in international journals, quality of research units). The Ministry of Higher Education and Research with the help of a dedicated team in charge of performance, organizes contracts for four years based on objectives for all the universities.

In addition to the requirement for universities, the Budget Directorate tries to encourage the use of performance data whenever possible. That is one reason why its performance team has introduced cross-cutting efficiency indicators, with more and more standardization, for support services. The directorate is benchmarking the costs of support services across line ministries in order to minimize costs. The main control factors are consolidation and standardization of purchases, professionalization of support functions, efficient use of office materials, and efficient property management. These are measured in terms of:

- the efficiency ratio of human resource management
- the office efficiency ratio (average annual direct cost of an office workstation)
- the efficiency of management of state property (an area ratio of m^2/agent and a ratio of servicing/area).

Some ministries also measure the cost of initial training.

The results of this type of benchmarking are relative, however, and can only support reduction of allocations in a system of program budgeting (with an overall envelope) rather than line item budgeting.

Problems of the Performance System

Capacity and Resources to Cover Transaction Costs

Since the LOLF was authorized, resources have been devoted to the reform. First, between 2003 and 2005 the Budgetary Reform Directorate was in charge of preparing for the introduction of the new performance budgeting system. After 2006 the Budget Directorate took on the new job of tracking performance for the CBA. Today a dedicated team of four or five civil servants is in charge of leading performance, working with a network of performance specialists in each line ministry. This team prepares the annual schedule for collecting performance data, drafts official documents related to performance budgeting, attends performance meetings with line ministries, leads line ministry working groups on management control, checks the quality of APPs and reports, and discusses these with stakeholders like the State Audit Office and the Parliament financial commission.

Performance, program budgeting, accrual accounting—that is to say, all aspects of new public management—are taught in civil service schools, such as ENA (*Ecole Nationale d'Administration*), the school for elite civil servants and members of the Court of Auditors, the Council of State, and inspectorates. Similarly, new methods of management are taught in civil servant continuing education programs: for example, the Budget Directorate has created an LOLF school (*l'école de la LOLF*) in partnership with the Institute of Public Management and Economic Development, which is the MoF training center. Its courses have enrolled hundreds of budget and operational unit managers, heads of services, and assistants. The courses are designed to give public managers an understanding of the main elements of the LOLF management system and to facilitate acquisition of the skills needed to meet new LOLF responsibilities.

However, it is still hard to say that major resources have been devoted to the reform. Because of the general budget constraints, allocating resources to performance is not really a priority. Yet the associated costs should not be overlooked. For one thing, it has created a managerial bureaucracy parallel to the traditional bureaucracy. Alain Lambert and Didier Migaud, who are proponents of the LOLF, themselves acknowledged in an October 2006 report that its implementation could produce "increased rigidity and a strengthening of constraints" in the preparation and conduct of budgets and lead to "de-motivation of managers." They proposed to introduce multiyear financing and reduce the number of programs and indicators (Lambert and Migaud 2006).

Too Many or Too Few Measures?

In 2006, the LOLF's first year, the APRs presented 650 objectives and 1,300 indicators for the general budget, though as previously noted, by 2015, these figures had been almost halved. The main reason for these large numbers is that France has chosen a mix of political objectives (outcomes), to be used for communication, and management objectives (quality and efficiency), that are useful for management control. Another reason is to avoid reducing program performance to one objective only. On average each program has 2.8 objectives, each with two indicators. But that is still too much for the stakeholders.

The Budget Department, which prefers efficiency indicators, tries year after year to reduce the numbers of indicators. With so many measures, line ministries find it hard to engage their ministers. For the Ministry of Education the number of indicators was close to 100 when the LOLF went into force; in the 2015 budget bill the number was down to 58. For the secondary education program, the number has dropped from 32 to 13.

Parliament itself is complaining about the amount of information, which has shot up since 2005. The number of budgetary document pages has increased from 3,500 for the last line-item budget to 14,000 today. Everything is available on the MoF website.

Data Trustworthiness
Line ministry data come mainly from the ministry statistics services, staffed by civil servants trained in the traditionally independent French Statistics Service, or from opinion polls that have been audited. But no one in either the line ministries or the Budget Department is in charge of checking data quality. This job has devolved to the CIAP, the independent structure of inspectors that guarantees the relevance and reliability of the information in the APPs. Criticisms were made about frequent changes of indicators in the early years of LOLF that were not clearly reported in the APPs.

Erosion of Political Support
The economic crisis that began in France in 2008 as a consequence of the Lehman Brothers failure and the subsequent sovereign debt crises have changed the priorities of the French government. Encouraging better performance has given way to the search for budgetary savings. Performance has not been abandoned but there are no more illusions about getting quick results. Support functions must be performed, but savings must be delivered. It is much more difficult in a yearly budget process to evaluate the results of operational policies, related, for example, to housing, the environment, health, transportation, and employment.

Moreover, members of Parliament do not actually use performance data to question civil servants. This lack of political interest from both the executive and the legislative branches is prejudicial to improving performance. That is why the Budget Department tries to reduce indicator numbers and to promote indicators of efficiency to link results with resources allocated.

Lack of Broader Change
The LOLF is a nonpartisan reform. But the economic crisis has blurred the meaning of new public management. The former, right-wing, government (2007–12 under President Sarkozy) established a merit-based salary system not only for high civil servants but also for middle management. Some part of the

allocation is given according to individual results (up to 20 percent for directors), and in some line ministries (Finance, Police), collective incentives have been developed.

The current, left-wing, government under President Hollande, pressured by trade unions, has modified the system for middle management, reducing the merit salary without using the words "merit" or "performance." Trade unions generally see "performance" as a way to save at the expense of civil servants.

Searching for performance means also seeking new methods of public management. The Sarkozy government entered into public-private partnerships (PPPs) for prisons, administrative buildings (Justice, Defense), and transportation (high-speed train lines); it also outsourced such services as procurement and maintenance of cars, maintenance of military helicopters, and training of military pilots. But some of the PPP and outsourcing decisions authorized by the MoF were taken without careful pre-assessment; the point of view was instead political (some would say "ideological: the private sector would perform better than the public sector). While retaining current projects, the Hollande government is more reluctant to practice outsourcing.

Absence of Cross-Cutting Goals
How cross-cutting issues are managed depends on the partner organizations. Central government programs usually represent the appropriations and goals related to the main public policies. Nevertheless, some public policies can be implemented by more than one line ministry and the appropriations located in several programs, such as road safety, overseas, city policy, international affairs, the fight against global warming, immigration and integration, women's rights, the fight against drugs, social integration, development assistance, regional development, state property, tourism, youth policy, civil security, and crime prevention.

To set out in detail the goals of policies whose appropriations are fragmented in different programs, the budgetary "cross-cutting policies document" contains the common goals and indicators for each public policy. This document, appended to the budget bill, also identifies the minister leader and the governance of the policy; but governance works only if there is a true organization: road safety is a good example because its goals are straightforward and it is governed by a dedicated committee chaired by the Prime Minister. For agencies identified as "operators," such as museums, universities, and research institutes, usually "performance contracts" between the central government and an operator set out appropriations and objectives for three or five years. The main objectives and indicators of operators that get budgeted subsidies are listed in their APPs. For some programs, such as meteorology, space research, and museums, subsidies represent almost 100 percent of program appropriations.

When responsibility for realizing public policies is shared by different public organizations—central government, operators, local authorities, social security institutions—it is almost impossible to formulate cross-cutting goals. For general public policies, such as health care, assistance for poor people, and environmental protection, the government can present general public goals but these policies are implemented by independent organizations, so that assigning accountability is not easy.

Variations in the Use of Performance Data

Defining indicators is more delicate in the public than in the private sector because it implies successfully measuring effects that do not necessarily translate as financial and it contradicts traditional control modes. To limit these negative effects, the role of performance indicators should be thought of not only in terms of control and incentives but also as topics for discussion and the exchange of good practices.

One famous example of measuring performance, raised early in the LOLF, is road safety, where the same indicator is used by both police and military forces: screening for the rate of alcohol while driving. To improve road safety, national police has set itself a higher rate—which suggests that controls are effective—and the military has sought a lower rate—which suggests that prevention is effective. The police have organized their controls throughout the day while the military concentrate their controls at night, close to nightclubs. Neither is wrong, but the manager of the road safety program must clarify how performance is to be measured.

The police use of performance data is often criticized because of strong communication from political leaders and its impact of citizens. There is a real risk of manipulation of the data to make results seem better, depending on the situation, such as by signs of activity by police services or refusing to register complaints. Some police officers say that hierarchical pressure is such that they can no longer distinguish between what is a real drop in crime and what is a fake.

With regard to justice, the objective "accelerate legal decisions" gives useful information of service quality for users, but for measuring it, the indicator "average duration of court decisions" is not entirely relevant and can produce perverse effects; it must be supplemented by measuring average length of time it takes to reach a judgment. Setting targets in this area is difficult and may have the effect that the simplest cases are preferred to substantive work. The nonautomatic link between output and outcome often creates a gap between political leaders and the public, who argue for results (outcomes), and public managers, who administer based on production (outputs).

Conclusion

In terms of the culture of the civil service the LOLF has been a success. The Financial Committee of the National Assembly (MILOLF) wrote in a 2011 report, "No doubt one of the most important successes of the LOLF after five years … is the dissemination of a performance culture and management in the French civil service, thanks to the chain of accountability." That same year the State Audit Office said in the tenth anniversary report, "The performance culture has been broadly disseminated among public servants." However, the latter report proposed some improvements:

- Merge performance and budgetary meetings in negotiations between line ministries and the Budget Department.
- Align objectives reported to Parliament with those that ministers assign to managers and to operators (agencies).
- Present only strategic objectives (outcomes) in support of the three-year central state budget, and reserve management objectives for APPs and APRs.
- Inform citizens of key results and performance.
- Link results to negotiation of budgetary resources.

All stakeholders recognized performance data as a democratic means of accountability to ensure the best use of public funds, responsive to The French Declaration of the Rights of Man and of the Citizen of 1789 in its article 15: "Society has the right to require of every public agent an account of his administration." Thus, it appears that a real cultural change has occurred, with true ownership by both national and local managers, who all accept the need to measure performance (outcomes) as well as activity (outputs).

The introduction of merit-based pay for public executives is a positive sign, but the most interest is in using performance data in management dialogue to understand results. This dialogue takes place between the national and the local levels and the results are tools for learning. There is also dialogue at the national level between program managers and financial and human resources directors. Finally, the program manager reports to the minister, and both report to the Parliament. This is the chain of responsibility and accountability.

Beyond the figures and simple observation of gaps between what was intended and what was realized, what matters is whether the analysis is relevant: whether the data are reliable; whether the action plan is practical; how well it is carried out; the impact of unanticipated events, positive or negative; and whether targets are too ambitious or not ambitious enough. Have performance indicators been a means of real mobilization for the administration? What is the quality of the management dialogue? Has there been a noticeable evolution toward "better spending"? What conclusions about medium-term targets and levers can be drawn for the future?

It is clear that improvements are needed in a number of areas, among them better selection of strategic mission indicators, standardization of efficiency indicators for support services, harmonization of common indicators for several programs, ways to check the reliability of measurements, and ensuring consistency of indicators over time.

The main challenge is to continue to reduce the number of indicators to guarantee that both ministers and members of Parliament have a better understanding of performance. There is not as yet enough political ownership by the executive or the legislature. Ownership can be enhanced by distinguishing indicators that belong in APPs and those that line ministries use for internal management purposes.

Lastly, the question of how to use performance data is still unresolved. It is true that there is not enough time for discussion of performance during budget negotiations; reducing the number of indicators can facilitate this discussion. But though it may be possible to link performance data and budgeting to efficiency and even quality indicators, how to use effectiveness indicators (outcomes) is still in question. This is true for most sovereign affairs. For instance, when the President of the French Republic decides to make war abroad to fight terrorists, he does not raise the question of value for money.

Performance budgeting is a gradual learning process. It takes time because it is iterative. In short, it is a continuous improvement process.

Note

1. The OECD has identified three types of performance budgeting: (1) Presentational performance budgeting: The publishing of performance information in budget and other government documents. This serves to disseminate information for greater transparency and accountability of government operations, but is not intended to play an explicit role in decision making. (2) Performance-informed budgeting: Either past or proposed future performance is used to inform decisions on the allocation of resources. Performance information is used along with other information in the decision-making process. (3) Formula performance budgeting: The allocation of resources based solely on past performance. Used only in specified sectors, such as education and health.

Bibliography

Abate, Bernard. 2002. "Les cibles de résultat sont elles utiles pour mieux gérer l'Etat." Revue Française de Finances Publiques, December.

Abate, Bernard. 2014. *La nouvelle gestion publique.* 2éme edition. Paris: LGDJ, Lextenso Editions.

Alventosa, Jean-Raphael. 2012. *Les outils du management public.* Paris: LGDJ collection Systèmes.

Arthuis, Jean. 2005. *LOLF: culte des indicateurs ou culture de la performance?* Senat Report. http://www.senat.fr/rap/r04-220/r04-220.html.

———. *Rapports de la commission des finances.* http://www.senat.fr/commission/fin/.

Bacache-Beauvallet, M. 2008. "Incitations et désincitations : les effets pervers des indicateurs." http://www.laviedesidees.fr.

Barilari, André. 2005. "La performance de l'État, mythe ou réalité." *Revue l'ENA hors les Murs,* May 2005.

———. 2011. "Le Comité interministériel d'audit des programmes : une occasion manquée?" *Revue française d'administration publique,* December.

Barilari, André, and Michel Bouvier. 2010. *La LOLF et la nouvelle gouvernance financière de l'Etat,* 3e ed. Paris: Lextenso, LGDJ Collection Systèmes.

Bezes, Philippe. 2009. *Réinventer l'Etat. Les réformes de l'administration française.* Paris: PUF: Collection "Le lien social."

Brunetiere, Jean-René. 2010. "Les objectifs et les indicateurs de la LOLF, quatre ans après…." *Revue française d'administration publique* 2010/3 (135).

———. 2006. "Les indicateurs de la loi organique relative aux lois de finances (LOLF): une occasion de débat démocratique?" *Revue française d'administration publique.* 2006/1 (117).

Chatelain Ponroy, Stéphanie, and Sponem Samuel. 2010. "Culture du résultat et pilotage par les indicateurs dans le secteur public." In *Management: enjeux de demain*, edited by Bernard Pras. Paris: Vuibert.

Conseil d'Analyse Economique. 2007. *Economie politique de la LOLF* (Arkwright et al., rapport du CAE N 65); *Performances, incitation et gestion publique* (Bureau et Mougeot, rapport du CAE N° 66). Paris: CAE.

Ecalle, François. 2011. "La LOLF, dix ans après." *Politiques publiques– Institut de l'entreprise.*

Englebert, Xavier. 2009. *Manager avec la LOLF : Pratiques de la nouvelle gestion publique,* 2ème edition. Paris: Revue fiduciai–e - Collection réforme de l'Etat.

Eyraud, Corinne. 2013. *Le capitalisme au cœur de l'Etat.* Paris: Editions le Croquant Collection dynamiques socio-économiques.

Felouzis, Georges. 2004. "Les indicateurs de performance des lycées, une analyse critique." *Revue Education et Formation* 70 (December).

Guillaume, Henri, Guillaume Dureau, and Frank Silvent. 2002. *Gestion publique–L'Etat et la performance.* Paris: Presses de Sciences Po et Dalloz.

Lambert, Alain, and Didier Migaud. 2006. "La Mise en Oeuvre de la Loi Organique Relative aux Lois de Finances: A l'epreuve de la pratique, insuffler une nouvelle dynamique a la reforme. Rapport au Government."

Ministry of Finance website on performance (managed by the Budget Directorate). 2015. *Some documents in English.* www.performance.gouv.fr. http://www.performance-publique.budget.gouv.fr/ressources-documentaires/documentation-en-anglais# .VKAt6ACkCA.

Ministry of National Education. *2013 data.* http://www.education.gouv.fr/statistiques. http://www.education.gouv.fr/cid57102/l-etat-de-l-ecole-32-indicateurs-sur-le -systeme-educatif-francais.html.

———. 2015. *2012 data in English.* http://cache.media.education.gouv.fr/file/etat23/57/9 /DEPP_EE_23_2013_english_316579.pdf.

Mordacq, Frank. 2011. "Premier bilan de la LOLF 5 ans après sa mise en œuvre." *Revue Française de Finances Publiques,* numéro 116, Mordacq, Frank. 2006. *La LOLF: un nouveau cadre pour réformer l'Etat.* Paris: LGDJ, Lextenso Editions.

———. 2009. *La réforme de l'Etat par l'audit.* Paris: LGDJ - Lextenso éditions.

———. 2014. *Les finances publiques,* 3ème édition. Paris: PUF – collection Que sais je?

National Assembly. "Annual reports of the National Assembly of the implementation of the LOLF." http://www.assemblee-nationale.fr/13/budget/milolf.asp.

———. *Rapports annuels de la commission des finances.* http://www.assemblee-nationale .fr/commissions/59048_tab.asp.

———. *Rapports de la mission d'évaluation et de contrôle.* http://www.assemblee-nationale .fr/14/budget/mec.asp.

Revue Française de Finances Publiques. 2002. N 77- 2002; Mettre en œuvre la LOLF- N° 86-2004; Nouvelle gouvernance financière publique — N 105-2009.

State Audit Office (Cour des Comptes). *Implementation of the LOLF 2001–2011* (with a summary in English). https://www.ccomptes.fr/Publications/Publications/La-mise-en-oeuvre-de-la-loi-organique-relative-aux-lois-de-finances-LOLF.

———. *Rapports annuels sur l'exécution (Budget Review Act annual reports)*. http://www.ccomptes.fr/.

Thelot, Claude. 1993. *L'évaluation du système éducatif*. Paris: Editions Nathan.

Trosa, Sylvie. 2007. *Vers un management post bureaucratique: La réforme de l'Etat, une réforme de la société*. Paris: L'Harmattan.

Trosa, Sylvie. 2010. "Performance et évaluation." *Gestion et finances publiques La Revue*, - N° 8-9 – Aout/Septembre.

Weiss, Jean-Pierre. 2009. *La division par zéro; essai de gestion et de mangement public*. Paris: Groupe revue fiduciaire.

CHAPTER 8

The Netherlands

Maarten de Jong

Introduction

This chapter looks at the performance budgeting efforts of the Netherlands and the lessons learned. The efforts have been managed by the Ministry of Finance (MoF) in cooperation with Parliament and the National Court of Audit.

The Dutch political landscape is a parliamentary democracy led by coalition governments and a high degree of decentralized power for line ministries. It can be argued that conditions have therefore been relatively unfavorable for a high-profile performance management initiative compared with, for example, France, whose government is more centralized. The Dutch Government Accounts Act grants the Minister of Finance the power to object to spending proposals because of the general budgetary situation or if a spending proposal is not expected to deliver enough value for money. As a result, decisions with budgetary consequences cannot bypass the MoF and be presented directly to the Cabinet or Parliament. Only the Cabinet can resolve a conflict between a line department and the MoF. Ultimately, then, the MoF has significant power to influence the spending of line ministries and to request information about the relevance, effectiveness, and efficiency of policy decisions (Schoch and Den Broeder 2013).

Performance Budgeting in the Netherlands

The Netherlands converted to performance budgeting between 1999 and 2002 and the system was revised between 2011 and 2013. The first performance budgeting wave not only sought to direct the focus to performance but also moved the budget from a traditional line-item to a program structure. In the latter each ministry allocates its expenditures by policy goals; the result is 5–15 policy articles per ministry. Each ministry also uses 2–3 nonpolicy articles for technical aspects, such as dividing residual overhead, unforeseen expenses, and fund transfers. Parliament bases its authorization of funds on these articles.

The OECD (2007) has characterized the performance budgeting process chosen by the Netherlands as a comprehensive top-down "big bang" approach. Performance planning has traditionally not been centralized. Other than integrating political priorities from the 4-year coalition agreements into their budgets, each line ministry is responsible for its own performance planning. Even within a ministry, the policy cycle seems to be largely disconnected from the pace of annual budgeting or the four-year coalition periods. Instead of a ministry-wide multiyear strategic plan, policies typically are appraised and adjusted at the end of a term set when a particular policy plan goes into effect, although sometimes a policy must be evaluated and redesigned in response to pressure from the media or changes in political preferences. To make sure that all policies are evaluated, the MoF oversees a comprehensive plan of policy reviews based on budget policy areas and annually selects a number of (often cross-cutting) policy areas for more elaborate spending reviews.

The 1999–2002 reforms were designed to integrate all financial and performance planning into the annual budget cycle, thus creating a single dominant process for both financial and performance planning and for accountability. Such a comprehensive approach proved overambitious, however, because diverse policy cycles were not easily integrated into a single process with a shared timeline. Nor was the budget able to accommodate and explain all relevant details for all policy areas without sacrificing readability and transparency. This suggested a potential tradeoff between the transparency of spending and reporting on performance.

The problems with the first wave of reforms led, between 2011 and 2013, to a more modest reform called *accountable budgeting* (De Jong, Van Beek, and Posthumus 2013). Major changes included simplification of the structure of policy articles, accommodation of more detailed information on financial instruments, separation of policy expenses from administrative expenses, and a more rigid policy evaluation structure. As explained in detail in the following section, the intent was to retain the advantages of the performance budgeting structure while making the budget more transparent and therefore more valuable.

Creating and Disseminating Data

The program budget structure is central to the annual MoF budget circulars and applies to all line ministries (see table 8.1). For nondepartmental agencies, a different format stresses efficiency indicators and financial accrual data.

Performance information can thus be included in two parts of the program structure (table 8.1): In the Role and Responsibility section indicators may apply to broad program outcomes and contextual factors (e.g., life expectancy for the public health program) and in the Explanation of Financial Instruments section indicators are linked directly to the number of beneficiaries of a financial instrument (e.g., the percentage of the target population participating in a national health screening program that receives a subsidy).

There is no requirement that indicators be included in every program budget. In fact, about a third of all policy articles in the 2014 budget had no indicators. In 2006, the MoF gave permission for performance indicators to be skipped if there was a satisfactory explanation of why it was impossible to find useful and relevant indicators. In 2011 the requirement for an explanation was

Table 8.1 Netherlands Ministry of Finance Program Budget Format

Budget format	Annual report format
General objective	
Express the purpose of the funding allocated for this program and the outcome desired	
Role and responsibility[a]	
Explain how the interventions of the Ministry can help achieve this outcome amid other stakeholders and external factors.	
Policy changes	**Policy conclusion and lessons learned**
Briefly explain the major changes from last year's budget.	Assess the degree of success of last year's policy realization and articulate lessons learned from evaluation, underperformance, or unexpected external events, if applicable.
Budget Table: Cash commitments, expenses, revenues (last two years and next four years in the budget and last four years in the annual report)	
Expenses are divided into 12 possible financial instruments, such as subsidies, income transfers to individuals, contributions to local government, independent agencies, international organizations, and purchases from the private sector. Within each category, the line department has to agree with the Ministry of Finance on the level of detail of any further specification.	
Explanation of financial instruments[a]	
For each line specified in the budget table, a brief explanation is offered of who receives funds through that financial instrument and their part in policy execution.	

Source: Based on RBV model 3.22, see www.rbv.minfin.nl.
a. Quantitative nonfinancial information can be found in these sections.

dropped but, as discussed below, was replaced by more stringent rules regarding the relevance of indicators. Examples of policy articles that lack indicators are those funding counter-terrorism, the meteorology service, and the financial contribution to the EU.

In its annual report, the MoF is expected to base its policy conclusion on the indicators specified and to offer explanations of any major difference between expected and realized results, with corrective measures described. The Policy Conclusion Statement not only interprets the performance information that is incorporated into the budget but also data to which the budget may refer, such as open data or evaluation reports. This section was for the first time included in all 2013 annual reports. The change reflected a concern that lists of numbers by themselves did little to draw external attention or inform internal analysis. While relatively recent, the early experience with policy conclusion statements indicates that ministries find it harder to clearly present their interpretation of performance data rather than just reporting a set of quantitative values. At times ministries may propose messages that seem at odds with their own indicators or evaluations. The MoF hopes nonetheless that by pushing ministries to provide meaningful information, the budget can contribute modestly to building up the government's capacity for learning and critical self-reflection.

In addition to the program formats, budgets and annual reports can cover key outcomes in the textual introduction to the documents. This is used to underline priorities and outcomes that cut across different programs. There is, however, no requirement for discussing indicators there.

Links to Other Forms of Budget Analysis

The Dutch system is characterized by multiple forms of analysis that rely to varying degrees on performance and evaluation information. Most prominent of these are spending reviews and policy reviews. Spending reviews are designed to support alternative policy and reform options and cut across programs, and often across ministries. Policy reviews are program-based ex post evaluations executed by a single ministry. Other types of ex post and ex ante evaluations that are planned and conducted by line ministries can be valuable inputs for the policy and spending reviews (Schoch and Den Broeder 2013).

Spending Reviews

The MoF has a tradition of undertaking cross-cutting reviews to identify possible spending cuts or alternative policy options—an approach lauded as a best practice in the international budgeting community (OECD 2007; Robinson 2013; Schick 2013).

Initially launched as *heroverweging*, reconsideration procedure, in 1981, spending reviews are carried out by groups consisting of MoF and spending department staff and independent researchers from the scientific community or a research or planning agency. A group is always chaired by someone seen as independent, often a former high civil servant or politician. Although the methodology and method have been largely unchanged in the past few decades, in the mid-1990s the emphasis of the reviews shifted from identifying potential budget cuts to identifying more general improvements in effectiveness and efficiency. Although a mandatory savings option may still be part of a particular review, requiring a savings option (often set at a minimum of 20 percent) for each review was dropped from 1995 on (Schoch and Den Broeder 2013).

The MoF annually presents the proposal for the next year's spending reviews at the Cabinet meeting that decides on that year's budget. In 2009 and 2010, in the aftermath of the fiscal crisis, an exceptionally comprehensive round of spending reviews was conducted with the explicit aim of finding options for budget cuts. This exercise covered about 75 percent of public spending, and many of the saving options recommended found their way into the platforms of political parties in the 2010 election (Schoch and Den Broeder 2013). Over the last three decades more than 270 spending reviews have taken place. The degree to which these reviews are performance-informed varies considerably but it seems to have clearly increased over time (Van Nispen and Klaassen 2010). Over the past decade, some elements of the successful tradition of spending reviews have been gradually blended into the performance budgeting process.

Policy Reviews

As early as 2004, the MoF concluded that the budget structure was best suited to increase transparency and that improvements in program effectiveness and efficiency would have to come from policy evaluation (IOFEZ 2004). However, policy reports to that date were judged to be subjective and of poor quality. This conclusion gave birth to a new evaluation tool, the *policy review* (*beleidsdoorlichting*), designed to overcome these problems; it was expected to impartially assess the purpose, necessity, and effects of a policy or instrument.

The policy reviews employ a set of standardized questions that ministries are expected to complete (table 8.2). Policy review reports are sent to Parliament together with a letter from the Council of Ministers that gives the Cabinet's assessment of the findings. The process is intended to take advantage of in-depth ministry knowledge but also ensure impartiality. The self-evaluation component is intended to encourage internal learning and reflection, avoiding a defensive response on the part of a ministry. Impartiality is facilitated by contracting with an independent expert to assess the responses and the methodology. The independent expert, the standardized questions, parliamentary oversight, and the involvement of the MoF are expected to ensure that reviews are sufficiently self-critical.

Since 2013, as part of the accountable budgeting reform, budget circulars mandate that each line ministry report when policy articles will be reviewed, reflecting the requirement that all policies be evaluated every four to seven years. The review schedule is made part of each ministry's annual budget, increasing the transparency of the process. The results of evaluations are expected to be summarized in the new Policy Conclusion Statements in the policy articles of annual reports.

Since policy reviews were introduced in 2006, they have been found to have a number of shortcomings (figure 8.1). For instance, policy reviews are often not conducted on schedule or are postponed (Von Meyenfeldt, Schrijvershof and Wilms 2008). Another criticism is that a significant number of policy reviews do not truly assess effectiveness (Von Meyenfeldt, Schrijvershof and Wilms 2008;

Table 8.2 Policy Review Questions

1.	Which (part of the) policy article and corresponding expenditures does the policy review assess?
2.	If applicable, when will other parts of the policy article be assessed?
3.	What was the reason for the policy intervention? Is the reason still valid?
4.	What is the responsibility of the central government?
5.	What is the nature and coherence of the instruments used?
6.	What are the expenditures for the policy, including related costs in other policy areas and programs?
7.	How are these expenditures substantiated? Can these be related to volume/use of services and prices and tariffs?
8.	Which evaluations of policy have been carried out? How have these evaluations been carried out?
9.	Which part of the policies has not been evaluated? If any, please indicate why certain policies cannot be evaluated.
10.	To what extent does the available research allow for judgment on the effectiveness and efficiency of the policy being reviewed?
11.	What impact and effects did the policy have? Were there any unintended consequences, positive or negative?
12.	How effective was the policy?
13.	How efficient was the policy?
14.	What measures can be taken to increase efficiency and effectiveness?[a]
15.	What policy options exist in case of a substantial drop in funding? (A drop of about 20 percent of funding for the policy article)[a]

Source: Schoch and Den Broeder 2013.
a. In effect as of January 1, 2015.

Figure 8.1 The Effectiveness of Outcome Goals: Breakdown of Evaluation Results, 2006–11, Representing €93.8 Billion of Annual Spending

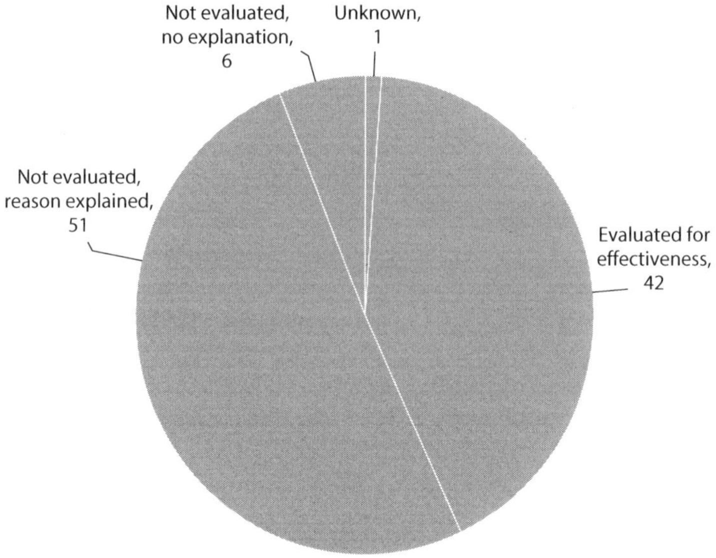

Source: Netherlands Court of Audit 2013.

Algemene Rekenkamer [Court of Audit] 2012, 2013). Parliament has also repeatedly expressed discontent with the quality, the quantity, and the usefulness of policy reviews.

The MoF has recently taken several steps to respond to these criticisms. It now presents the progress of line ministries in policy review planning twice a year to the Council of Ministers, and the ministers must explain any delays to Parliament. Also, since 2015 two additional questions have been added to policy reviews that explicitly address efficiency and effectiveness and identify potential areas for savings (table 8.2). In addition, the schedule for policy reviews will also state the central question and the intended data sets to be used. The changes respond to criticism that reviews did not address the questions for which Members of Parliament (MPs) would like answers.

As can be seen in figure 8.2, the increased emphasis on policy reviews and the measures taken recently appear to be increasing the number of reviews conducted. It is hoped that this will better enable Parliament to fulfill its oversight role and use its budget authorization power to demand necessary changes in programming and the content of policy reviews well in advance.

Changes in Performance Budgeting over Time

The history of performance budgeting in the Netherlands can be traced back at least 40 years. However, only during the last 15 years has it taken the shape of governmentwide reforms. Four different phases can be distinguished (figure 8.3).

Figure 8.2 Policy Reviews Sent to Parliament, 2006–14

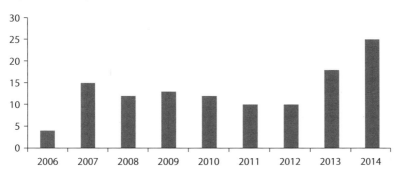

Source: Netherlands Ministry of Finance, www.rijksbegroting.nl.

Figure 8.3 Performance Budgeting in the Netherlands, 1970s–Present

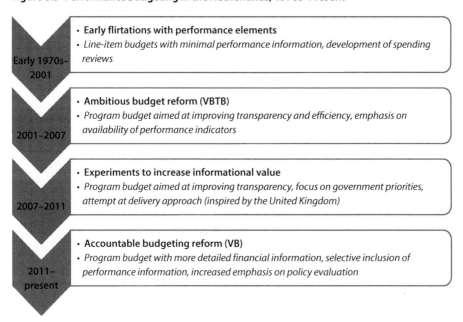

Note: The years dividing the periods are not as arbitrary as they may appear. In reality, there were transitional periods between phases of two or three years.

Early Flirtations with Performance Elements (early 1970s–2001)

Impressed by the U.S. Planning, Programming, and Budgeting System (PPBS), in the early 1970s the Netherlands MoF appointed a commission for the development of policy analysis. Although this commission pioneered much of the thinking about performance and evaluation issues in the Netherlands, at the time none of its work was institutionalized in the budget process, and in 1982 it was abolished (Schild et al. 2002). Some early signs of a performance-based approach to budgeting emerged in the 1980s. One was the institutionalization of spending reviews, induced by the fiscal climate at the time. Another was that a provision in the Government Accounts Act stated that performance information should be included in budget documents "if possible and useful" (Schild et al. 2002). As a result, some performance indicators could be found in the budget texts preceding the line items, but it was still impossible to relate these metrics systematically to any budgeted expenses.

Ambitious Budget Reform (2001–07)

After a few decades of cautious experimentation, at the turn of the century the Netherlands turned to performance-based program budgeting. Under the acronym VBTB (*Van Beleidsbegroting tot Beleidsverantwoording*), translated as Policy Budgets and Policy Accountability), the traditional structure of the federal budget was extensively revised to become performance-based. The new structure was intended to enhance transparency, efficiency, and the effectiveness of government spending while allowing ministry managers more flexibility. Although the emphasis in early documents primarily stressed enhanced budget transparency, from the start the reform also aimed at improving the efficiency of allocation and the results orientation of public entities (Van der Knaap 2001).

VBTB moved the budget from a traditional line-item document to a program budget where funds are authorized according to general policy objectives. At the heart of the performance budget were three simple questions that required an answer for each government spending choice and needed to be laid down in budget programs (table 8.3).

The logic and simple appeal of these questions was valued greatly for building and enhancing performance dialogue as part of the budgetary process. In combination with extensive capacity-building and communication initiatives, the MoF made a point of consistently indoctrinating financial and policy staff in these questions.

The program budget reform was viewed as a logical consequence of prior reforms that placed responsibility for both resources and policy in the hands of ministry managers. The structure was intended to align accountability for both spending and results (Debets 2007). The reform was deeply motivated by New Public Management theories that had already led to agentification[1] and conversion to accrual accounting for decentralized parts of the government.

The VBTB reform also sought to look for ways to raise the profile of performance. One approach was to introduce a new milestone in the Netherlands budget calendar: an annual Accountability Day in May. On this day, the Minister of Finance presents to Parliament the central government annual financial report

Table 8.3 Questions from VBTB Reform That Applied to All Programs

Budget	Annual Report
What do we want to achieve?	Did we achieve what we intended?
What will we do to achieve it?	Did we do what we meant to do?
What will be the costs?	Did it cost what we expected?

and the annual reports of the other ministries. It was expected that assigning a fixed day in the budget calendar for looking back at policy results would stimulate a dialogue between the administration and Parliament about the effectiveness and efficiency of public spending—and indeed, the ceremonial presentation of the budget in September traditionally draws considerable attention from MPs and the media.

When VBTB was evaluated in 2004, its main positive results were considered to be the greater accessibility and readability of budget documents. Moreover, the explicit dialogue on measurable goals and performance values did appear to improve the results orientation of ministries (IOFEZ 2004). Although hard to substantiate, the latter point is in line with other findings on the effects of introducing performance budgeting in OECD countries (GAO 04–38 2004; OECD 2007).

Experiments to Increase Informational Value (2007–12)

The difficulties with VBTB were exemplified by the fact that the new Accountability Day continued to draw only limited attention from Parliament. The turnout of MPs was modest, and the budget debates had little connection to the policy content of the annual reports. On the 2007 Accountability Day the mutual discontent was debated to the point that the administration and Parliament agreed that changes had to be made or the idea of Accountability Day would have to be abandoned. The discontent centered on three issues:

- Political attention to accountability for results was still too limited.
- The annual reports focused too much on technical details and too little on political relevance.
- The links between past results and future plans was not clear.

In the years that followed, an experiment was conducted to deal with the perceived problems of earlier performance reforms, and also to decrease the administrative burden of performance budgeting requirements on line ministries. The experiment made some substantial changes in annual reporting, particularly by giving priority to the policy priorities of the government's coalition agreement rather than reporting on all government activities. In reporting on the priorities, a Lessons Learned section was added.

Some ministries eliminated all policy information (text and performance indicators) from the budget,[2] in the hope of reducing technical details that were of little interest to policymakers or usefulness for results accountability. A policy review was to accompany each annual report sent to Parliament to trigger debate about the effectiveness, efficiency, and usefulness of programs.

A new instrument introduced as part of this experiment was the Accountability Letter, in which the Prime Minister reported to Parliament on progress on the Cabinet's main priorities. This letter accompanied the annual reports. To ensure maximum attention to these reports, Parliament selects a small number of policy themes six months before Accountability Day. This priority-driven approach to annual reporting coincided with the enthusiasm of the government at the time for the U.K.'s experience with the Prime Minister's Delivery Unit during the second term of Prime Minister Tony Blair. In the Netherlands, the Ministry of General Affairs (the equivalent of the U.K. PM Office) handled monitoring and assessment of progress and scheduled talks between the PM and line ministers if progress was not sufficient. The MoF was closely involved with external reporting about priority goals because that was aligned with the budget process.

A major barrier to the Netherlands version of the British approach was the absence of an equivalent strong central institution at the heart of government. Moreover, the priority goals specified in the coalition agreement amounted to no less than 84, some of which were vague, politically formulated, and lacking a clear strategy for achievement. Another difference from the British approach was that although the Blair government in adopting this tool emphasized internal management, in the Netherlands it was set up as a strategy for external accountability. This heightened the tendency to politicize the reporting of results (De Jong, Van Beek, and Posthumus 2013). A study by the Parliament budget office in 2008 concluded that although 80 percent of the performance information in the budgets and annual reports referred to policy objectives in the coalition agreement, less than 40 percent demonstrate cleard and accountable results (BOR 2009).

When the MoF evaluated these experiments in 2011, it concluded that while more selective reporting on priorities did to some extent increase political attention to results, the problems of the relevance of performance information and the high ministry workloads were for all practical purposes unsolved (MoF 2011). Parliament did not give more attention to policy reviews when they were released simultaneously with the annual report. On the contrary, MPs indicated that the policy reviews were buried by the vast amount of information in the annual reports. When debating annual reports, MPs rarely referred to the performance indicators that had been omitted from them (De Jong, Van Beek, and Posthumus 2013).

Of the experimental measures, the Prime Minister's Accountability Letter was retained, as was the notion that the annual reports should incorporate a policy conclusion and a lessons learned statement. Perhaps more important, by observing what worked in the experiments and what did not, the MoF acquired a keener appreciation of the value of performance information. This knowledge would be put to use in the next reform.

Accountable Budgeting Reform (2012–present)
The period of experimentation saw explicit discussion by all stakeholders—especially the MoF—of problems with performance budgeting and what to do next. Among the options were returning to previous methods or abandoning program budgeting altogether and returning to the line-item budgets of the previous century. The 2009/2010 round of comprehensive spending reviews turned out to be pivotal: MoF staff working on the reviews found out how little value the current budgets had for financial analysis in general and for formulating

options for 20 percent spending cuts in particular. The Great Recession also increased the need of Parliament for input-oriented financial information, especially about the government's administrative expenses. The coalition government had vowed to cut these costs but at the time they were not presented clearly in the budgets.

The insights gained and the pressures of the Great Recession resulted in a comprehensive reform of performance budgeting. "Accountable budgeting" was intended to retain the advantages of program budgeting while toning down unrealistic expectations about how performance data would be used. More input information was put into the budgets but inclusion of performance information was more selective. In addition, there was more emphasis on comprehensive and systematic policy reviews as the primary tool for assessing policy effectiveness.

The MoF recognized that the variety of government interventions did not justify a one-size-fits-all link between funding and results but suggested that performance data could also be used in a variety of other ways. The VBTB idea of aligning results accountability with financial responsibility was upheld for a minority of cases where government itself is the dominant party in financing and executing activities directed to a particular outcome on society, and external factors have little effect on the outcome (government *executes* in figure 8.4). An example is preventing major floods by maintaining the coastline. For this policy objective the outputs (reinforcement of the coast measured in cubic meters of sand deposited by the infrastructure agency) have a fairly straightforward causal connection with the outcomes (maintaining the norm for the percent of minor overflows of the present coastline). In such cases an output or outcome target can truly be regarded as a promise to deliver results in return for funding. The MoF pointed out that government fulfills a variety of more passive (government *finances*) or marginal (government *stimulates*) roles, sometimes nonfinancial (government *regulates*). In these cases performance accountability is limited and performance information is more informative for clarifying the policy context or substantiating funding levels.

Figure 8.4 Roles of the Government of the Netherlands in Policy Programs

Source: Netherlands Ministry of Finance.

Toward Next-Generation Performance Budgeting · http://dx.doi.org/10.1596/978-1-4648-0954-5

The additional specificity about the type of government intervention led to budget documents that were more clear and more factual. The length of ministerial budget documents was reduced by about 30 percent (De Kam 2012) and about 50 percent of the performance indicators disappeared from the documents (De Jong, Van Beek, and Posthumus. 2013). The MoF also saw more questions from Parliament about the effectiveness of specific financial instruments and about multiyear fluctuations in specific budget estimates. As a result, the MoF has concluded that the accountable budgeting reform strengthened the connection between policy and spending in budget documentation (MoF 2014).

Besides taking a more selective approach to presenting performance information and offering more detail in specifying program expenses, the accountable budgeting reform required a more transparent presentation of organizational expenses (running costs). The need for budget cuts after 2008 directed political attention to such issues as salaries, external hiring, and information technology. The structure of the budget at the time did not allow for monitoring these expenses, which were collected in a single nonpolicy article rather than allocated to separate policy areas. The new reform also introduced uniform definitions of organizational expenses. Comparable information from annual reports allowed the Ministry of Internal Affairs to issue an annual account based on organizational expenses across ministries and nonfinancial targets relating to efficiency measures.

The new presentation of organizational expenses and the selective approach to performance indicators was a somewhat counterintuitive approach to traditional performance budgeting logic. These parts of the reform required a substantial effort to convince some stakeholders, notably the Court of Audit and several line ministries.

As the external auditor of the annual reports of the line ministries, the National Court of Audit had been supportive of the VBTB reform but was more hesitant in its support of the accountable budgeting reforms. The Court has persistently emphasized the availability of performance indicators in relation to issues like usefulness and validity. After initially expressing support for the 2007–11 accountability experiments, it was soon criticizing the resultant loss of information to Parliament. The new approach sent a somewhat confusing message to employees of line ministries as well. For over a decade the MoF had pressed them for performance indicators; now they were told to include only indicators that were useful for external accountability or that helped substantiate funding levels.

The accountable budgeting reform saw the MoF arguably turn against some of the New Public Management philosophy that had largely characterized performance budgeting in the Netherlands (Van Hofwegen and De Jong 2012). At the same time, centralizing the organization expenses of a line ministry into a single article per ministry also provided new flexibilities consistent with New Public Management. According to the program budget structure, personnel could now be transferred to different programs and projects within a line ministry without having to submit budget reallocation proposals to Parliament.

However, this also meant that the different units within a line ministry could no longer count on the program structure to shield their portion of organization costs from cuts.

Some at the MoF viewed abandoning mandated comprehensive coverage of spending with performance indicators as a rejection of the performance budgeting ideal. What is clear is that expectations that outcomes could be related to government expenditure were adjusted downward. This shift to a more pragmatic approach, which did not happen overnight, offered important advantages:

1. It allowed the debate on performance indicators to shift the focus from the availability of performance information and compliance to one more centered on the quality and usefulness of indicators. During VBTB auditors criticized annual reports for failing to have enough output and outcome indicators, which created a powerful political incentive to set measures for all spending areas. The MoF came to realize that the growing number of indicators, often of dubious relevance, was not making the budget more useful.
2. The changes were intended to reduce ministry use of performance information for advocacy purposes. Since performance budgeting requires government entities to present evidence that they are performing, it is not surprising that in a political environment performance data can easily become a means of advocacy (Moynihan 2008)—and tempt them to present results or promise targets that are beyond their control. As the MoF categorized policies in terms of degree of government control (see figure 8.4), it became less feasible for ministries to promise outcomes or claim credit for functions in which they took no part. Reducing the amount of performance data in the budget also reduced incentives for ministries to frame the data for political purposes. Presumably, data that no longer belong in the budget but are used for policy design or program management will survive their expulsion from the budget and continue to be used. As stakeholders often consider these data to be relevant, ministries are encouraged to make them publicly available in an open data format.

The shift to a more modest approach to performance indicators was possible only because in the previous decade government had experienced the shortcomings of the rigid comprehensive approach. At the same time the VBTB era that preceded the current approach can be credited with drawing the attention of civil servants to evidence-based policy and helped to promote a performance dialogue. The decade of VBTB reform also fostered a growing cultural belief within government that the use of indicators for policy design and internal program management is expected to underlie ministry spending.

The Netherlands experience is also a reminder that the budget is inevitably a highly political document. Using it as the mechanism to consider performance issues makes the selection and appraisal of performance information vulnerable to political framing. Another lesson is that there is no clear correlation between mandating indicators in the budget and policymaker use of the data – if anything the relevance of performance data to budget decisions seems to have gone up since they have been used more selectively in the budget.

Use of Performance Information
Governmentwide Use

There is no evidence that performance indicators have had a significant role in the political debate about allocations during budget authorization. Their use in negotiations between the MoF and line ministries is also relatively rare (OECD 2014). Since 2013 Parliament has shown growing attention to policy reviews—though the MoF sees reviews as garnering little interest; most of it comes from the Budget Committee and is largely concerned with the procedure for reviews rather than their actual content.

The MoF sees performance indicators discussed somewhat more often within line ministries. When critically assessing the financial consequences of proposed policy plans beforehand, the Financial and Economic Affairs Directorate (FEAD) in each ministry often challenges policy staff to make their assumptions about expected effectiveness and efficiency as explicit as possible. FEAD staff use the information available on effectiveness and efficiency to underpin their arguments for reallocating funds within ministries. Figure 8.5 shows the results of a 2013 MoF questionnaire about the activities of FEAD staff. Of these, policy effectiveness and efficiency, as well as evaluation, can be expected to be most associated with use of performance information. These activities cumulatively represent an estimated quarter of FEAD activities within ministries.

It appears that to varying degrees there is a performance dialogue between policy directorates and independent agencies. In some cases, considerable effort is invested in annual agency plans and quasi-contracts between line ministries and agencies, yet these are referred to only sporadically in a mostly ritual dialogue. In others, performance indicators from integrated performance and financial plans are frequently discussed. In some cases the loss of specialist policy knowledge in line ministries in recent years has made such discussions more difficult (De Jong and Van Nispen 2014). Although there has been no governmentwide study, use of performance information is believed to be considerably higher within executive agencies than at the ministerial level. For example, over 75 percent of respondents to a questionnaire within the Netherlands Forest Service indicated that they rely on performance information in their work (De Jong 2013).

As for use of the results of spending reviews, MoF respondents indicate that they are occasionally used directly in drafting coalition agreements or in budget negotiations. More commonly, however, they are used internally to explore potential saving options. These options may not be referred to for many years but then become part of a budget negotiation or funding proposal (Van Nispen 1993). A similar pattern applies to policy reviews and other evaluations, and there is also evidence, though sparse, of evaluations being used directly for program learning, with favorable budgetary consequences.

Figure 8.5 Activities of Line Ministry Financial Economic Affairs Departments
percent

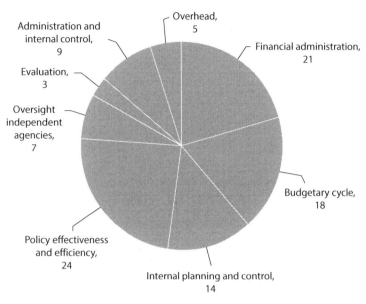

Source: Netherlands Ministry of Finance.

Ministry of Finance Use

According to respondents from the MoF, performance information is seldom used directly in budgetary negotiations with the line ministries. Evidence from evaluations or other reports is used occasionally to support arguments during the budget process but may remain on the shelf for years before becoming relevant. For example, the impact of a spending review of primary and secondary education, part of the round of comprehensive spending reviews in 2009/10, seems to have been substantial. The report explored five options that could save from €0.6 to €4.1 billion. Although the radical spending cuts proposed did not occur then, many of the measures proposed were adopted a few years later.

Though a number of austerity packages were passed, the education budget remained relatively unscathed. Protecting education was championed by one opposition party whose support was needed for cuts elsewhere—an experience that illustrates the priority of political preferences over performance evidence in determining aggregate funding.

Parliament Use

For a long time, Parliament made limited or no use of performance information in budgets or annual reports. When MPs do mention performance indicators, they generally refer to issues of indicator availability and quality and not to actual policy content using the reported values. Education is one policy area where Parliament has recently demonstrated an unusual appetite for performance data. The Education Commission assessed education performance while discussing both the Ministry of Education, Culture, and Science 2014 budget and its 2013 report. Combining the figures provided by the ministry with those from international institutes and the media, two committee members made detailed presentations of performance data to their colleagues and the minister. Parliamentary debates on both the 2014 budget and the 2013 annual report were preceded by a substantial number of performance-related questions and resulted in several votes related to the ministry's performance.

A close examination provides evidence at odds with the stereotype of the Ministry of Education, Culture, and Science as disconnected from schools. While the reliance on per pupil funding limits the use of financial incentives to encourage schools—at one point causing the National Court of Audit to compare the ministry to an oil tanker that was hardly able to turn itself in another direction if required—the ministry has in small but significant ways heightened attention to performance data.

Difficulties with the Performance System

Capacity and Resources

The increased administrative burdens arising from measuring and reporting performance were recognized soon after performance budgeting was introduced (IOFEZ 2004). One persistent frustration shared by staff at line ministries has been that MPs consistently ignore the work they put into the performance-based annual reports. Given the shrinking numbers of financial staff, the administrative burden has been central to later attempts to reform the system. Although unable to entirely eliminate the perception of pointless bureaucracy, the reduction of policy texts and indicators has reportedly helped to significantly ease ministry workloads.

Substantial resources were devoted to VBTB; an unofficial MoF estimate is €180 million to train the staff of line ministries. The accountable budgeting reform took far less resources, reflecting its more modest character and the general capacity constraints that arose after the fiscal crisis.

Too Many or Too Few Measures?

Too many performance measures and too little relevance were the main reasons for VBTB reform. Even the more selective accountable budgeting approach saw 1,000 indicators, 50 percent of the total, removed from budget documents between 2011 and 2013. Some of these remained valuable for managing internal performance and monitoring policy trends within a ministry or agency, but others, introduced primarily to comply with budgeting requirements at the time, had little or no informational value.

Data Trustworthiness

The reliability of performance data was viewed as an issue in the earlier years of performance budgeting. In response to questions from Parliament and critical reports from the Court of Audit, there was pressure on the MoF to issue elaborate regulations to safeguard reliability. The MoF refrained from doing so, fearing an excessive bureaucratic burden (IOFEZ 2004). Instead it required line departments to explicitly state the source of the performance data in their budgets and have an auditable process of collection so that selected performance data could be audited randomly.

Erosion of Political Support

The introduction of VBTB in 1999–2002 was championed by an influential Finance Minister and supported by the Court of Audit and several well-informed MPs. The gradual shift away from these reforms began with a new Finance Minister in 2007. Meanwhile, apart from occasional requests for particular performance data, MPs have been indifferent. Examples of MPs actively engaging in analysis of performance data and challenging ministers with their findings, as in the education case, are quite rare.

Absence of Cross-Cutting Goals

The problem of silos in performance accountability surfaced during the experience with the Dutch version of the Blair PM delivery unit. For a few goals of the coalition government, responsibility was to be shared by different ministries. This clearly confused line ministries when the accountability process was aligned with the budgetary system, which centered on ministerial allocations. In some cases ministries started pointing at each other or responsibility shifted back and forth over time. Attempts have also been made to put together groups of project staff from different line ministries to tackle policy issues that cut across ministries (e.g., youth). Generally, this structure was not seen as successful; it seemed to simply result in more silos. Ad hoc spending review boards have been more successful in tackling cross-cutting policy goals.

Perverse Use of Performance Data

With direct financial incentives to achieve performance targets being quite rare, there have been no high-profile cases of outright fraud, but more subtle cases of data manipulation have been reported. One example is the incorrect registration by some schools of the education level of parents in order to be eligible for extra funding. In another case the national railroad company improved its punctuality performance in response to financial incentives, apparently by rearranging its timetables at the expense of passenger transfer time. Other examples of undesirable effects were cases where performance targets were met by cherry-picking the workload by selecting the cases that required the least effort (e.g., reactivation of the jobless) or apparently perpetuating a problem in order to keep receiving extra funding (e.g., waiting lists in hospitals). Perhaps some of this behavior would have occurred with or without a performance budgeting system. However, the emphasis on accountability for measurable results seems likely to have aggravated it.

Toward Next-Generation Performance Budgeting • http://dx.doi.org/10.1596/978-1-4648-0954-5

Conclusion

The Netherlands at first enthusiastically pursued a comprehensive performance-based budgeting reform. Benefitting from strong political support and substantial communication and capacity-building efforts, large areas of the public sector were effectively indoctrinated in the philosophy of results orientation and accountability. Soon after, a combination of disappointment and limited political interest prompted revision of the approach. The second wave of reforms was characterized by less performance data, more emphasis on finance in the budget, and greater reliance on policy evaluation to assess program effectiveness and efficiency. The more modest current system seems to better fit the needs of Parliament, the line ministries, and the MoF.

Notes

1. "Agentification," a core element of New Public Management, involves breaking down traditional bureaucracies into separate autonomous agencies to increase efficiency and effectiveness in the public sector.
2. In the annual reports at the time, progress on government priorities was described in a separate section and policy articles were treated as the main concern.

Bibliography

Algemene Rekenkamer. 2012. *Effectiviteitsonderzoek bij de rijksoverheid* [Research into Government Effectiveness]. The Hague: Court of Audit.

———. 2013. *Effectiviteitsonderzoek bij de rijksoverheid: Vervolgonderzoek.* [Further research into government effectiveness] The Hague: Court of Audit.

Bordewijk, Paul, and Henk Klaassen. 2011. *Begroten met Beleid - pleidooi voor planning en control op maat bij de gemeenten* [Budgeting with Policy – Plea for Planning and Control Tailored to Municipalities]. The Hague: Handboek Publiek Management, sdu Uitgevers.

BOR (Bureau Onderzoek en Rijksuitgaven). 2009. *Voortgang van het experiment verbetering verantwoording en Begroting* [Progress of the Experiment in Improving Accountability and Budget]. Tweede Kamer der Staten Generaal Nr 09-BOR-N-017.

De Jong, M. 2013. "Using Performance Metrics in Public Sector Agencies to Learn and Improve: A Matter of Institutional History and Identity?" Paper presented at the Public Management Research Conference, Madison, WI, June 20–22.

De Jong, M., I. Van Beek, and R. Posthumus. 2013. "Introducing Accountable Budgeting: Lessons from a Decade of Performance-based Budgeting in the Netherlands." *OECD Journal on Budgeting* 12 (3): 1–34.

De Jong, M., and Frans K. M. Van Nispen. 2014. "On the Utilization of Performance Information in Times of Austerity: From Success to a Return to Squeaky Wheel Budgeting?" Paper presented at the Association for Budgeting and Financial Management Conference, Grand Rapids, MI, October 1–3, 2014.

De Kam, C. A. 2012. "Nieuwe wijn in nieuwe zakken—Enkele kanttekeningen bij Verantwoord Begroten" [New Wine in New Bags—A Few Caveats for Accountable Budgeting]. In *Jaarboek Overheidsfinanciën 2012*, edited by J.H.M. Donders and C.A. de Kam. The Hague: Sdu Uitgevers.

Debets, Raphael. 2007. "Performance Budgeting in the Netherlands." *OECD Journal on Budgeting* 7 (4): 103–22.

GAO 04–38 (2004). *Results Oriented Government: GPRA has established a Solid Foundation for Achieving Greater Results.* Report to Congressional Requesters. Washington, DC: General Accounting Office.

IOFEZ (Interministerial Consultations for Financial and Economic Affairs). 2004. *Policy Budgets and Policy Accountability: Evaluation – Lessons from Practice* (Self Evaluation of NL Performance Budgeting Effort by Ministries).

MoF (Ministry of Finance). 2011. "Brief aan de Tweede Kamer der Staten Generaal" [Letter to the Lower House of Parliament]. (TK Vergaderjaar 2011–2012, 31865, No. 36). The Hague: MoF.

———. 2014. "Brief aan de Tweede Kamer der Staten Generaal" [Letter to the Lower House of Parliament]. TK Vergaderjaar 2014–2015, 31 865, No. 65. The Hague: MoF.

Moynihan, Donald P. 2008. *The Dynamics of Performance Management – Constructing Information and Reform.* Washington, DC: Georgetown University Press.

OECD 2007. *Performance Budgeting in OECD Countries.* Paris: OECD Publishing.

———. 2014. *Budgeting Practices and Procedures in OECD Countries.* Paris: OECD Publishing.

Robinson, Marc. 2013. "Spending Reviews." Paper prepared for the 34th Annual Meeting of OECD Senior Budget Officials, Paris, June 3–4.

Schick, A. 2013. "The Metamorphosis of Performance Budgeting." Paper prepared for the 34th Annual Meeting of OECD Senior Budget Officials, Paris, June 3–4.

Schild, Jan, Harmen Hoekstra, Peter van der Knaap, William Lelieveldt, and Hans Monnickendam. 2002. *Boter bij de Vis, 65 jaar Begrotingszaken, 200 jaar begroten* [65th Anniversary of Budget Affairs Directorate, 200 Years of Budgeting]. The Hague: Ministry of Finance.

Schoch, M., and C. den Broeder. 2013. "Linking Information on Policy Effectiveness to Budget Decisions in the Netherlands." *OECD Journal on Budgeting* 3: 1–22.

Van der Knaap, P. 2001. "Beleidsevaluatie en VBTB: Een nieuwe aanpak voor de rijksoverheid" [Policy and VBTB: A New Approach to Government]. *Openbare Uitgaven* 33 (6): 252–64.

Van Hofwegen, Joost van, and Maarten de Jong. 2012. "Naar een verantwoorde begrotings-presentatie - Over verantwoord omgaan met (on)zekerheden" [Toward an Accountable Budget Presentation]. In *De toekomst van de financiële functie van het Rijk: een beeld voor 2020.* [*Future of Government Finance: A Vision for 2020*]. 74–90. The Hague: Ministry of Finance.

Van Nispen, Frans K. M. 1993. *Het dossier Heroverweging* [*The Reconsideration File*]. Delft: Eburon.

Van Nispen, Frans K. M., and H. L. Klaassen. 2010. "Heroverweging: Een beleidsanalytische manier van bezuinigen" [Reconsideration: A Policy Analytical Way of Making Cutbacks]. *TPC: Journal for Public Governance, Audit and Control* 8 (4): 4–10.

Von Meyenfeldt, Lone, Carlien Schrijvershof, and Peter Wilms. 2008. *Tussenevaluatie Beleidsdoorlichting.* [Preliminary Evaluation of Policy Review Tool]. Evaluation study conducted by Aarts De Jong Wilms Goudriaan Public Economics by (APE) for the Netherlands Ministry of Finance, The Hague.

CHAPTER 9

Poland

Maarten de Jong

Introduction

The cities of Cracow and Szczecin used performance budgets successfully in the mid-1990s, and for the last decade performance budgeting has been on Poland's national agenda. The EU also suggested that results-oriented budgeting be made a priority for public finance reform when it assessed the Polish convergence program (Kęsek and Weber 2009).

The first national initiative was launched in 2006 with the aim of having a pilot scheme for the 2008 and 2009 budgets, a traditional-plus-performance budget in 2010, and a performance budget by 2011. After a change of government in 2007, responsibility for performance budgeting was moved from the Chancellery of the Prime Minister to the Ministry of Finance (MoF). At that point political support abated and the pace originally envisaged slowed (Allam 2008).

Arguably, the MoF has not been in a good position to implement such a far-reaching governmentwide reform. Although those responsible at the MoF have been persistent and ingenious, the Polish reform has been criticized as being disconnected from the heart of government. Its detailed and ambitious structure has also been criticized for ignoring the fact that in large areas of the public sector there is no performance management culture, so that progress has been slow and the impact minimal (Kęsek and Weber 2009; Hardt and DeJong 2011; OECD 2013). However, the MoF Public Finance Reform Department (PFRD) succeeded in finishing the performance budget structure and may be ready to deal with the difficult challenge of enhancing the use of performance information. Some recent organizational reforms at the MoF, the ambition to merge Poland's traditional and performance budget structures, and the initiative to pilot spending reviews could all provide support for using performance information in budgeting.

Performance Budgeting in Poland

Creating and Disseminating Data

The legal foundations for Poland's performance budgeting requirements were established in the 2009 Public Finance Act. The act makes the MoF responsible for the effective and efficient execution of the budget (Art. 174). Units that oversee parts are tasked with supervision and control of the realization of performance plans and with enforcing preventive and corrective action (Art. 175). In addition, the Council of Ministers must submit a performance-based accountability report (Art. 182) to Parliament and the Court of Audit. The law also assigned a prominent role to a new position, the National Coordinator for the Performance Budget (Art. 95). The first coordinator resigned in 2010, however, and two years later the function was discontinued.

The performance budget covers all government activities and spending except for local governments and the national health fund. The system has a hierarchical structure that distinguishes four levels: functions at the top, then tasks, subtasks, and activities. Objectives and indicators are defined for the last three. The MoF requires that up to two targets be identified for each task and that each organizational entity engaged in a task include its single most important indicator in the performance budget. The performance budget has some 5,000 to 6,000 indicators. Internal planning and management of performance by ministries uses a uniform template for all levels of the performance budget classification (table 9.1). Specific targets must be proposed, and the unit responsible identified.

The performance budget is an annex to the legally binding traditional budget, which is based on organizational units. This may have been intended

Table 9.1 Performance Indicator Card

1. Code Task / name of the item: _____	2. Target: _____
3. Name of the measure: _____	
4. Justification for the choice of the measure: _____	
5. The calculation algorithm of the measure: _____	
6. Unit of measurement: _____	7. Source of data for the measure /sub-measure: _____
8. Measure used in previous years Yes / No	8a. Reasons for changes in the measure and the possible difference in methodology in comparison to the previous period (in case of 'No'): _____
9. The terms of measurement (data availability) Measure mode: Continuous (current) / Periodic Measurement frequency: Monthly / Quarterly / Bi-annual / Annual / Other / Explain	
10. Values Base value Expected performance Plan Forecast 2012 or _____ 2013 2014 2015 _____ _____ _____ _____ **Preferred trend values of the measure:** Descending / Ascending / Stable	
11. Risk of not meeting the target: _____	12. Comments: _____
13. Leading organizational unit responsible for the realization of the measure: _____	
14. Approved by budget holder or person authorized in this regard Date and Signature: _____	

Source: www.mf.gov.pl, Zal_66_Karta miernika.

to be a temporary phase until the traditional budget was replaced by a performance-based budget (Hawkesworth, von Trapp, and Nielsen 2011), but the division remains. The fact that two separate budget classifications coexist has been problematic for implementing performance budgeting in Poland. Because the classical budget is still legally binding, it continues to be the one on which ministries and parliament focus. The differences are shown in table 9.2.

When annual budget requests are submitted, they must be supported by performance data. After evaluating the requests, the MoF issues letters to ministries that set spending caps for the coming year. The MoF staff tasked with the performance budget must resolve the problem of matching funding and performance planning by combining the two budgets. Although its staff is highly skilled and experienced, the capacity available at the MoF limits how systematically this is done. In fact, the requests are selectively scrutinized based on such factors as budgetary significance, political attention to certain issues, and the experience of previous years.

Beyond the budget preparation phase there are two other formal moments in the budget cycle that call for the MoF and line ministries to interact over the performance budget. In early July, line ministries send midyear reports to the MoF, and in the annual account ministries report their progress for the entire year.

The 2009 Public Finance Act also introduced the Multi-Year Financial Plan (MYFP). This three-year framework is based on the 22 functions identified in the

Table 9.2 Classical and Performance-Based Budgets Compared

Traditional budget structure	Example	Performance-based budget structure	Example
Parts (84)	Ministries, institutions, EU funds, local government grants, debt servicing	Functions (22)	Main policy areas such as Function 3: education, upbringing and care or Function 6: state economic policy
Sections (33)	Activities/areas such as industry; agriculture or transport	Tasks (145)	Main programs such as 4.4 public debt management; 6.1 increase of competiveness of economy
Chapters (576)	Subareas regarding sectors such as industry, agriculture or transport	Subtasks (698)	Subprograms such as 6.1.3 creating conditions for increasing the innovativeness of enterprises
Paragraphs (229)	Economic classifications such as wages or investment	Actions (< 4 000)	Subactivities such as 6.1.3.1 creating conditions for functioning of enterprises

Source: OECD 2013.
Note: Numbers are based on the 2010 budget.

performance budget and sets deficit and debt thresholds. Linking the two budgets, it translates appropriations from the traditional budget into expenditures according to the performance budgeting structure. Ministers must annually submit to the MoF information about how they are implementing the MYFP and progress toward achieving their objectives. This information is then submitted to the Council of Ministers and published. Because this practice came into effect only recently, it is too early to assess its impact, but in terms of allocations it is likely to be limited (OECD 2013).

In addition to its connection to the MYFP, the performance budgeting structure is also linked to strategic planning because targets from Poland's National Development Strategy 2020 (NDS) are linked to tasks from the structure. The connection is quite weak, however, because only a limited percentage of government activities and spending is affected by the NDS priorities.

A technical limitation is that the two different budget classifications obscure whether reallocations in the legally binding traditional budget are or are not performance-informed. The Polish system is characterized by relatively more budget flexibility for line ministries than in other OECD countries (Hawkesworth, von Trapp, and Nielsen 2011). Poland is also one of only 10 OECD countries that have fewer than 300 line items in the budget (OECD 2014). This means that ministries have considerable discretion in reallocating funds within the traditional line items. This loosens connections between performance data and decisions, though ministries have the discretion to build such connections as needed.

The definition of performance budgeting for Poland as explained in Article 2 of the 2009 Public Finance Act reflects elements of both program budgeting and performance management:

A performance system is the statement of expenditures of the state budget or the costs of a public sector entity prepared in accordance with state functions, representing various areas of state activities, and:

a) grouping the tasks of budget expenditure by objective;
b) grouping subtasks and actions to achieve the objectives of the task;

along with a description of the objectives of these tasks and subtasks, as well as the baseline and target indicators of the objectives of the state, specifying the value, quantitative or descriptive character of the base and target level of outputs from inputs.

Reformers acknowledged that adopting performance management would require major changes to the entire Polish civil service (Postula and Perczynski 2010). Despite the government's capacity-building and training efforts, many civil servants are not aware of the logic underlying performance budgeting and continue to view their role as traditional administrators rather than project managers. They see risks in being held accountable for results but few rewards even if they achieve their targets (Hardt and De Jong 2011).

The conditionality attached to the EU structural funds required more strategic planning and coordination to achieve the objectives identified in the strategic plans, but although this intensified external pressure, Poland has not yet fully internalized these new practices or extended them to management of domestic funds (OECD 2013).

The fact that agencies continue to rely on the traditional budget as the legally binding method for financial allocation and authorization has made it easy for them to disregard performance information in making budget decisions. The fact that the two budget systems are still disconnected and have so far existed as separate silos has exacerbated this problem. Analyses by the Court of Audit in 2011 and 2012 showed that formal application of the performance budgeting method did not significantly change the budget process: ministries continued to focus on the spending limits set by the legally binding budget (Mislag 2013).

Links to Other Forms of Budget Analysis
In terms of the OECD performance budgeting typology, the Polish system should be characterized as presentational performance budgeting rather than performance-informed budgeting or direct formula performance budgeting (Postula 2013). Although the use of performance information for budget allocation is very limited, the performance budgeting system did help the MoF conduct better examinations of public spending, and the traditional budget system was useful for maintaining budget discipline (Hawkesworth, von Trapp, and Nielsen 2011). This suggests that performance budgeting is used to some extent as an analytical tool.

While ex-post evaluation of policy is used for EU-funded programs as well as in assessing the legality of acts, it is not commonly used as a financial tool. Unlike most OECD countries, in Poland current regulations do not mandate that the MoF carry out spending reviews. Only new initiatives are subjected to scrutiny, not programs already in existence (Hawkesworth, von Trapp, and Nielsen 2011).

Nonetheless, in 2014 after a major reorganization a new evaluation unit was set up, the Expenditure Policy Department. One of its responsibilities is to conduct spending reviews. As part of this mandate the unit intends to simplify and restructure the performance classification of expenditures to make it more useful in spending reviews. In cooperation with the MoF and with OECD and World Bank support, it is piloting spending reviews in the areas of social spending and financial policy. The initiative is a response to recommendations from Brussels related to the EC's excessive debt procedure for member states. The MoF assumes that the analyses of the effectiveness of state spending will be taken into account during work on the draft budget act for 2016 (MoF 2014). It has yet to be seen how much these spending reviews will be focused on performance rather than being merely legalistic.

Beyond the lack of a formal tradition of ex post policy evaluation, a more serious obstacle may be that the Polish civil service lacks a results-oriented culture and learning routines. Performance budgeting and performance management techniques treat civil servants as providers of services to the public and base evaluations on performance targets and indicators (Kęsek and Weber 2009).

In Poland, as in many other countries, the public sector has no pattern of critical self-reflection or of using performance measures and stakeholder feedback as opportunities to learn and improve.

Arguably, the Ministry of Regional Development (MRD), which was merged into the Ministry of Infrastructure Development in 2013, should have had a strong interest in evaluating performance because it is responsible for EU-funded programs, which the EU requires that it systematically monitor and evaluate. But MRD staff do not differ much from peers in other ministries in terms of their knowledge of targets, indicators, and the national performance budgeting reform effort. The general disregard of the system was reflected in the comments of a senior MRD official, who said, "Our goal is to spend money.... What we really need are better evaluations, and not the performance budget imposed on us by the MoF" (Hardt and De Jong 2011).

Performance Budgeting Changes over Time

The design of the Polish system has been fairly consistent since its creation. The OECD, which advised Poland on performance budgeting, concluded that, despite some shortcomings, its approach is in line with other EU countries and provides a sound foundation for moving forward (OECD 2013).

The reform called for "preparation of a system allowing for the introduction of an activity-based budget managed by results" (Hardt and De Jong 2011). This dual objective of introducing a system of both activity-based and performance budgeting is reflected in the system's ambitious design. In fact, in Poland the activity-based budget is often used as a synonym for the performance budget. The activity-based performance budgeting classification has, for example, resulted in the choice to assign specialized schools for the military or agriculture to the education task rather than the army or agriculture. The design of the Polish system explicitly recognized that activities may contribute to more than one goal. However, this can make attribution of and accountability for results quite complex.

One clear technical challenge is the repetition of objectives with the same content for different elements or classification levels. This can obscure the attribution of activities to subtasks and of subtasks to tasks. To diminish not only these problems but also the administrative burden and to make the performance budget more understandable, the large number of tasks and subtasks in the performance budget has been cut significantly in recent years. For example, the number of subtasks was brought down from a peak of 698 in 2010 to 353 in the 2013 budget (Postula 2013).

Not unlike other performance budgeting systems, the quality and usefulness of Poland's indicators has been another concern. Generally, positive examples come from policy areas with a relatively straightforward relationship between activities and outcomes, such as safety and traffic. Moreover, in the Polish system, there seems to have been a tendency to choose aggregate, but not necessarily relevant, indicators in order to cover all the operations of a particular entity (Hawkesworth, von Trapp, and Nielsen 2011). Throughout the years, gradual refinements have been made (Postula 2013) to change activities and targets from those that were more administrative and descriptive (e.g., "processing applications") to ones that are more results- and impact-oriented (e.g., "'shortening waiting time"). A technical difficulty addressed in the last few years was that certain funds were counted twice during financial consolidation because they were transferred between government entities.

Although no radical changes have yet been made to the system, that may be about to change. In 2014 the Minister of Finance proposed merging the parallel budget classifications. The original aim had been for the performance budget to replace the traditional budget as the legally binding document. After a long period of uncertainty about the complexities of the dual budget situation and about its future, the original ambition seems to have been abandoned; the ministry's more modest ambition now is to integrate performance data into the traditional budget. As one senior MoF respondent eloquently put it: "After eight years of trying a revolutionary approach, we … are ready now to follow an evolutionary strategy instead" (interview January 14, 2015).

Adoption of the Current System

When the performance budgeting initiative was launched in 2006 it was the responsibility of the Chancellery of the Prime Minister (CPM). Teresa Lubinska was appointed state secretary at the CPM to lead the budget reforms. A scholar and former Finance Minister, Professor Lubinska was not only respected but also had direct experience with successful performance budgeting as a member of the city council in Szczecin. Within the CPM, a new unit with a staff of seven, the Department of State Performance Budget, was supported by the European Social Fund (Allam 2008).

EU pressure was a pivotal factor in the initial stage of the reform. Not only was performance budgeting introduced in response to EC recommendations for public finance reform, Poland also needed budget reforms if it was to avoid the EU excessive deficit procedure. Indeed, performance budgeting was promoted as a tool to facilitate fiscal consolidation. For these reasons, at the time the reform was high on the agenda of the Kaczynski government (Hardt and De Jong 2011).

A change of government in 2007 initially did not seem to signal serious changes to the performance budgeting reform. In 2008, however, it was decided to move the Department of State Performance Budget from the CPM to the MoF, where it became part of the Public Finance Reform Department (Słodowa 2013). Some saw this as a way to institutionalize performance budgeting in a more stable and less politicized institution (Allam 2008) and also make it more relevant to actual budget decisions.

However, the relative weakness of the MoF has eroded some of the benefits of making performance budgeting its responsibility. MoF scrutiny of spending by line ministries seems to be underdeveloped (OECD 2013). Authority for the traditional budget authority is fragmented between five separate MoF departments (OECD 2014), and the move of performance budgeting to the MoF is likely to have undermined contact between performance budgeting reformers and other ministries, as well as the ability to directly influence implementation efforts. Moreover, this move disconnected the performance budgeting operation from the strategic thinking at the heart of government. (Hardt and De Jong 2011; Słodowa 2013). It seems clear that the performance budgeting reform never fully recovered from the loss of its comfortable position at the center of power and of the support of a political champion like Professor Lubinska.

Despite a loss of political support, PFRD continued to demonstrate its commitment to performance budgeting (see table 9.3). Thanks to the unrelenting efforts of its staff and leadership, implementation of technical performance budgeting aspects has proceeded at a relatively steady pace. However, the final step of replacing the traditional budget with the performance budgeting structure has become ever less certain.

Not surprisingly, different parts of the Polish government have had different responses to performance budgeting reform. The Ministries of Health and National Education led the reform. The Ministry of Defense is also cited as an enthusiastic adopter. Managers in Defense and National Education saw a clear link between the performance budgeting structure and their actual tasks and operations (Hawkesworth, von Trapp, and Nielsen 2011). More generally, the MoF saw the organizations that had been working longer with advanced management information systems as the most reliable, though sometimes stubborn, partners in getting performance budgeting started.

Opposition from civil servants stemmed from the fact that preparing the performance budget entailed extra work in addition to preparing the traditional budget (Allam 2008). The reform had no legally binding consequences, and the lack of general reform of the public sector raised doubt that such traditional problems as lack of coordination would be resolved. Moreover, the results in terms of transparency and program learning were also seen as disappointing (Słodowa 2013). Civil servants had little influence in designing the reform, and their lack of buy-in was recognized as an obstacle early on.

Table 9.3 Chronology of Performance Budgeting in Poland

Budget year	Status of PB reform
2007	Pilot for 28 science and 38 higher education functions
2008	PB structure covers 44% of state budget spending
2009	PB covers 100% of state budget spending
2010	PB covers 100% state budget spending and of 14 extra-budgetary public finance entities
2011	PB covers 100% of state budget spending and of all extra-budgetary public finance entities except the National Heath Fund and local government entities
2012 and 2013	Presentation of a comprehensive performance budget parallel to the traditional budget
	Performance budget gains additional legal status as provisions on mid-term reporting and budget supervision and control of effectiveness by budget holders came into effect

Sources: Allam 2008, Hawkesworth, von Trapp, and Nielsen 2011; Postula 2013.

The EU paid for training in activity-based and performance budgeting for thousands of government employees, though some criticized the lack of follow-up to the training effort (Mislag 2013), and capacity problems remain. Among these are limited resources and little time spent on personnel issues, chronic politicization of senior staff, and lack of incentives to retain competent staff (Kęsek and Weber 2009). (Concerning the last, it should be noted that, unlike in many other CEE countries, in Poland civil servants are generally not undercompensated compared to staff in the private sector.)

Some of the resistance of civil servants to performance budgeting is better understood from a historical perspective: A trademark of the post-communist era in Poland was a desire to separate politics from administration that resulted in the "autonomization" of public administration. Administrators may have seen the reforms as an effort by political actors to reassert their control and reduce administrative independence (Staniszkis 2001; Hardt and de Jong 2011).

Use of Performance Information

Governmentwide Use

Poland still does not have a performance management culture. Moreover, the Polish civil service has been characterized as a collection of dispersed and often autonomous government entities with little cooperation and coordination between or even within them (Kęsek and Weber 2009; Hawkesworth, von Trapp, and Nielsen 2011; Hardt and De Jong 2011). Performance is not widely managed and performance agreements or contracts with agencies and managers are rare. There are few incentives, formal or informal, for civil servants to actively undertake such reforms.

Despite the existing MoF routine of reviewing performance targets and tracking progress, the results are seldom used in dialogue with line ministries. The processes for planning and reporting on performance budgeting are mostly concentrated in the State Budget Department's performance budgeting unit, which is the successor to the PFRD, but other units are responsible for interaction with line ministries over allocations.

When budgets are being prepared, line ministries are most likely to refer to performance information when proposing additional spending or policy reforms, but otherwise performance seldom affects allocations. More funding is sometimes followed by an upward adjustment of targets because of MoF pressure, but if targets are not met consequences for a line ministry or agency are rare. Mid-year reporting occasionally does lead to questions being asked of line ministries if progress is lagging. The Court of Audit has commented on the performance budgeting system but has so far refrained from doing performance audits.

Sometimes members of Parliament ask questions about the performance budget annex to the annual report. In some respects, Poland has the conditions necessary for thorough parliamentary oversight of the budget. The budget calendar allows enough time for members to scrutinize proposals, and Parliament has independent analytical capacity (Hawkesworth, von Trapp, and Nielsen 2011). Moreover, Parliament authorizes relatively few line items in the traditional budget. This gives ministries and agencies the flexibility to engage in performance-informed reallocation without political micromanagement.

As noted, the process and the results of working with performance information vary greatly by ministry and agency. For some agencies, the value of performance budgeting has been proven, and over time more public entities are expected to find it useful (Hawkesworth, von Trapp, and Nielsen 2011). Among the anecdotal and mixed evidence on government use of performance information, it appears that the Ministry of National Education (MNE) perceives the process of defining indicators and targets as contributing to its internal management. MNE senior managers even view performance budgeting as having introduced useful new information and a new way of thinking about policy preparation and execution. Performance budgeting has also been credited with improving the understanding and presentation of MNE's work (Hawkesworth, von Trapp, and Nielsen 2011).

Difficulties with the Performance System

Capacity and Resources

As the performance budgeting reform was set up in part to respond to EU recommendations, its operation initially enjoyed substantial EU financial support. This support was used to set up the management unit in the CPM and for large capacity-building programs. Nevertheless, the time and resources needed to implement performance budgeting processes have generated opposition within the civil service. The minimal capacity of the MoF to monitor and assess performance information is reported to be an additional bottleneck.

Too Many or Too Few Measures

Due to its activity-based structure and intended comprehensive coverage, the Polish performance budgeting reform has struggled with an overload of measures. In recent years, there have therefore been attempts to simplify the structure and slim down the number of measures. As a result, between 2010 and 2013 the number of performance budgeting subtasks was roughly halved—but the number of indicators is still seen as too high.

Trust in Data

The Court of Audit has criticized the fact that setting measures, measurement, and reporting the results are all left to the discretion of ministries and agencies themselves as undermining the credibility of reported performance (NIK 2012; Mislag 2013). The MoF, however, claims that the reliability and quality of the information are safeguarded by random Court audits. (Given the limited use of the information generated by the performance budgeting system, so far this issue mainly draws attention from technical experts.)

Erosion of Political Support

The active and powerful political support the performance budgeting reform at first enjoyed under Professor Lubinska did not carry over into the next two administrations. Although Poland never formally backed away from the reforms, it was clear that they were losing political priority. Examples are the transfer of responsibility from the CPM to the MoF and the fact that the intention to replace the traditional budget with the performance budget was never really reiterated. The OECD identified this lack of political support as a major threat: "If political support is not forthcoming, performance budgeting will wither away and become a paper exercise which will not add value to the Polish public sector" (Hawkesworth, von Trapp, and Nielsen 2011).

Moving from Measuring Data to Using it

During budget preparation, performance data are used only in specific areas and even there only sporadically. Nor has there been any attempt to use it in reforming the internal management of line ministries (Hawkesworth, von Trapp, and Nielsen 2011). Poland is still at an early stage in using performance information and has no real performance management culture. However, using their own databases some ministries and agencies do use performance information systematically in formulating and monitoring policy. Poland is currently piloting spending reviews, but the extent to which these will be performance-informed and evidence-based is not clear.

Lack of Broader Change

Lack of changes to Poland's public sector generally is seen as a barrier to effective performance budgeting reform, in particular the lack of incentives to embrace modern management by objective methods but also the disconnection of the performance budgeting system from strategic planning (Hardt and de Jong 2011; OECD 2013). Additional challenges arise from the fragmentation of the MoF and the existence of two parallel budgets, with the traditional budget the one that is legally binding. On the other hand, the circumstances in terms of budgetary oversight and managerial flexibility in Poland seem supportive of the aim of performance budgeting reform.

Absence of Cross-Cutting Goals

The intricate design of the Polish performance budgeting structure anticipated the tension between vertical budget accountability and the reality of goals that cut across different organizations and fields of responsibility. The structure chosen therefore allows for a function or task that is the responsibility of a single minister to be executed with the help of budget holders in other ministries. This allows for a hierarchical budget presentation whatever the organizational structure. However, such cross-cutting budget responsibility can also blur the accountability of organizations and jeopardize flexibility because each reallocation may require the agreement of multiple budget holders (Hawkesworth, von Trapp, and Nielsen 2011). Partial misalignment between performance budgeting financial accountability and accountability for results is further complicated by the fact that the traditional, and legally binding, budget allocations are based on an entirely different classification system.

Conclusion

In spite of difficult circumstances, about a decade ago Poland launched an ambitious performance budgeting reform. Soon afterward the powerful political support with which it began diminished. An organizational move from the powerful Chancellery of the Prime Minister to the relatively fragmented MoF complicated implementation, as did the coexistence of two parallel budget classifications and the lack of a broader reform agenda that could have stimulated a performance culture throughout the government. Undiscouraged by these adverse factors, the MoF unit responsible showed remarkable determination in designing a performance budgeting system modeled on OECD best practices. However, the reform was criticized as being disconnected from strategic thinking in government and there was a lack of buy-in not only from politicians but also from the civil service and civil society. Nevertheless, development of the system is credited with stimulating the use of performance information by some ministries and agencies.

At present the performance budgeting unit functions as a rather solitary intelligence unit covering budget effectiveness and efficiency. The challenge continues to be how it can disseminate the knowledge it gathers for broader use in decision making. Doing this systematically, with the budget process as the linchpin, proved too ambitious even without impediments specific to Poland. The current goal of merging the two parallel budget systems and enriching the traditional system with performance information is more modest but seems more realistic. Another recent development has been the piloting of spending reviews that build to some extent on performance budgeting. Both approaches seem to signal a shift to an evolutionary approach.

Poland's current budgeting system arose partly from EU pressure for budget discipline. The country's latest report to the EU on its fiscal consolidation effort makes no mention of its performance budgeting reforms. This may reflect not only Poland's adjusted reform expectations but also those of the entire performance budgeting community. The Polish example illustrates what can happen when state-of-the-art performance budgeting reform is consistently pursued in a public sector that in many respects was not yet ready for it.

Bibliography

Allam, Miriam. 2008. "The Development of Performance Budgeting in Poland." Paper presented at the expert meeting sponsored by the study group on Public Sector Financial Management of the European Group for Public Administration, Vienna June 4–5, 2008.

Council of Ministers, Poland. 2012. *National Development Strategy 2020—Active Society, Competitive Economy, Efficient State*. Attachment to Resolution No. 157 of the Council of Ministers, September 25.

Hardt, Ł., and M. de Jong. 2011. "Improving the Quality of Governance in Poland through Performance Based Budgeting." Program Sprawne państwo [Better Government Programme], Ernst & Young, Warsaw. Report presented on December 7, 2011.

Hawkesworth, Ian, Lisa von Trapp, and David Fjord Nielsen. 2011. "Performance Budgeting in Poland: An OECD Review." *OECD Journal on Budgeting* 2011 (1): 7–57.

Kasek, L., and D. Webber. 2009. *Performance Based Budgeting and Medium-Term Expenditure Frameworks in Emerging Europe.* Warsaw: World Bank.

Ministry of Finance. 2014. *Report on Action Taken by Poland in Response to the Council Recommendation of 10 December 2013 in order to bring an end to the situation of an excessive deficit.* Warsaw.

Misiąg, Wojciech. 2013. "Siedem lat wdrażania budżetu zadaniowego—refleksje i prognozy" [Seven Years of Implementation of Performance Budgeting—Reflections and Forecasts]. *In Studia BAS Nr 1*, edited by Kamilli Marchewki-Bartkowiak and Zofii Szpringer, 85–102. Report to Parliament. Wroclaw: Chancellery of the Sejm, PAN.

NIK. 2012. *Wdrażanie budżetu państwa w układzie zadaniowym—Ocena procesów: planowania, monitorowania i sprawozdawczość* [Implementation of the Task-based Budget—Evaluation Processes: Planning, Monitoring, and Reporting]. Audit report. KAP-4101-01/2011, Nr ewid. 27/2012/P/11/001/KAP), Warsaw May 2012.

OECD. 2013. *Poland: Implementing Strategic-State Capability.* OECD Public Governance Reviews. Paris: OECD Publishing. http://dx.doi.org/10.1787/9789264201811-en.

———. 2014. *Budgeting Practices and Procedures in OECD Countries.* Paris: OECD Publishing. http://dx.doi.org/10.1787/9789264059696-en.

Postula, Marta. 2013. *Budżet zadaniowy w Polsce—osiągnięcia i wyzwania* [Performance Budget in Poland—Achievements and Challenges]. In *Studia BAS Nr 1* (33), edited by Kamilli Marchewki-Bartkowiak and Zofii Szpringer, 59–85. Report to Parliament. Wroclaw: Chancellery of the Sejm, PAN.

———. 2014. "Performance Budgeting in School Education in Poland." Paper presented at the 10th annual meeting of the OECD Senior Budget Officials Performance and Results Network. Paris, November 24–25.

Postuła, Marta, and Piotr Perczyński. eds. 2010. *Performance Budgeting in Poland.* Warsaw: Ministry of Finance.

Słodowa, Małgorzata Hełpa. 2013. *Budżet zadaniowy w systemie zintegrowanego zarządzania rozwojem—możliwości, dylematy, obaw* [Performance Budget System Integrated Development Management—Opportunities, Dilemmas, Fears]. In *Studia BAS Nr 1(33)*, edited by Kamilli Marchewki-Bartkowiak and Zofii Szpringer, 126. Report to Parliament. Wroclaw: Chancellery of the Sejm, PAN.

Staniszkis, J. 2001. *Postkomunizm* [Post Communism]. Gdańsk: Słowo/obraz terytoria.

CHAPTER 10

Russian Federation

Ekaterina Vaksova

Introduction

This study reviews how performance budgeting has been implemented in the Russian Federation. Despite the perceived value of performance budgeting, tracking the relationship between planned outputs and the needed resources is not easy. Russia has adopted a form of program budgeting, with goals and measures tied to programs. Its introduction has triggered a number of important changes in the modus operandi of executive authorities, the quality of their deliverables, the skills of their staff, and their understanding of the situation in their own sectors. As Russia has seen, it takes more than a decade to redesign a country's budget and move it to performance budgeting. The process was accompanied by other reforms, of administration, budget institutions, the budget accounting system, and the education finance system among others.

Overview

In Russia performance budgeting has been evolving for more than 10 years. The changes in core system parameters may be traced by looking at the Russian policy documents that describe the main programmatic instruments (discussed in the following Historical Background section):

- 2004: The 2004–06 Concept of Fiscal Reform in Russia, from which emerged the Register of Expenditure Mandates, Reports on Outputs and Key Areas of Business, and agency-targeted programs. This was the first attempt to introduce a new ideology: a transition from expenditure planning to outcome planning.
- 2010: The Government Program to Enhance the Effectiveness of Budget Expenditures till 2012, adopted by Government Directive №1101-p of June 30, 2010. This program drew attention to the fact that strategic planning and budget planning were not well-linked. One of the main tasks was to identify mechanisms to ensure better integration of strategic and budget planning and to monitor the achievement of stated objectives.

- 2013: The Program on Enhancing the Efficiency of Budget Spending till 2018, which was a comprehensive introduction to programmatic budgeting.

Technically, the development and conduct of government programs of Russia are regulated by the Ministry of Economic Development (MoED), which, with the Ministry of Finance (MoF), draws up and approves methodological recommendations.

The centerpiece of the current system is the design and conduct of government programs by Russia (regions and municipalities also design programs). Based on the subject matter, the 42 government programs are grouped as follows: new quality of life (13), innovation and modernization (17), national security (2), balanced regional development (6), and effective government (4). Although regional and municipal programs generally mimic the titles and structure of government programs, they are fewer because their responsibilities are narrower and more specific. The government programs serve as the fundamental instrument of programmatic budgeting in Russia, aligning budget resources with socioeconomic indicators and government performance indicators.

Initially the general list of government programs was designed in compliance with the goals and indicators specified in the 2020 Concept of Long-Term Socioeconomic Development of Russia, approved in November 2008. Later, Federal Law №172-FZ of June 28, 2014, *On Strategic Planning in the Russian Federation* structured the system of policy documents that define the basic socioeconomic objectives and plans:

- The President's Annual Address to the Federal Assembly of Russia
- The Socioeconomic Development Strategy of Russia
- Sector strategic planning documents
- Medium- to Long-term Socioeconomic Forecast of Russia
- Key Areas of Business of the Government of Russia.

Performance indicators for executive authorities are set in the six-year action plans that guide them as they implement or co-implement the strategic plans they are responsible for; these set out objectives, areas of business, targets, and planned interim and final outputs. Indicators of government programs are aligned with those in the Key Areas of Business document.

The federal law *On Strategic Planning* was enacted to prescribe coordination of public strategic management and fiscal policies; outline the powers and responsibilities of federal, regional, and municipal government authorities; and set out procedures for their interaction in the area of strategic planning with nongovernmental, academic, and other organizations. This law refers government programs to strategic planning documents designed to be part of planning and programming at the federal, regional, and municipal levels.

The legal underpinning for the design of government programs is the List of Government Programs in Russia, adopted by Government Resolution №1950-p of November 11, 2010. The list contains the titles of the 42 programs and the line ministry or agency responsible for each. According to Government Regulation №588 of August 2, 2010, and later amendments, the MoED and the MoF prepare the list of programs based on federal laws, resolutions of the President and of the Government of Russia, and suggestions from other ministries.

The authorities, from line ministries as well as the MoED and the MoF, first attempted to prepare government programs guided by the Federal Law on the 2012 Federal Budget and the Planned Period of 2013–2014. The work schedule for preparing the 2011 draft federal budget and corresponding documents for 2012 and the planned period of 2013 and 2014 set deadlines for preparation, review, and adoption of government programs.

Because not all the agencies responsible were equally prepared to draft government programs, the MoED, in coordination with the MoF, in 2011 adopted provisional rules that gave them options to prepare draft programs either as full-fledged programs meeting all the regulatory requirements[1] or in the form of abridged key provisions (concepts) that met[2] a limited number of requirements for sections and attachments. Since the second option made it easier to meet the tight deadlines, many ministries and agencies opted for it.

Between 2012 and 2014 the government of Russia adopted 39 programs.

For the first time, the 2014 federal budget and the planned period of 2015 and 2016 were aligned with the programs adopted. In the spring and summer of 2014, the government amended its program documents to capture the 2012 May 7th Presidential decree specifying priority measures to improve public policy across key sectors, such as education, science, health care, social, economic, demographic, and foreign policy; military service, defense, interethnic concord, public administration, and comfortable housing and utilities. The decrees contain specific requirements, quantitative indicators, and deadlines. By 2014, government programs had captured 55 indicators listed in the May decrees. The programs added 88 supplementary indicators to facilitate achievement of the mandates set out in the decrees. Also, the parameters of government programs were revised to match the President's Budget Address for 2014–16.

All programs are subject to public consultations and preliminary discussions at the meetings of civic councils held by the agency responsible.[3] The programs are adopted by the Government of Russia and contain the following sections[4].

- Government program key facts sheet
- Subprogram key facts sheets
- Federal targeted programs key facts sheet[5]
- Government program priorities and objectives, including general requirements of regional policies in a given area, such as the involvement of a specified subnational government in implementation of the federal program
- List and features of the key actions for the targeted program, such as deadlines for completion and expected outcomes, and links between actions, outputs, targets, and government program indicators

- List of regulatory measures that support achievement of the goal or expected outcomes of the program, with key provisions and deadlines for adopting needed regulations
- List of key indicators and government program indicators with annual planned targets, and with actions and outputs aligned with indicators
- Information on the sources of financing of the program from the federal budget and extra-budgetary funds of Russia
- Federal spending ceilings for long-term government contracts to implement key actions for the government program
- Rules for federal budget subsidies to subnational governments to further the government program
- Plan for implementation of the government program for the following fiscal year and the entire planning period.

Also, government programs must be accompanied by supplementary information and analytical and supporting documents that are not subject to adoption, including the outlook for the area covered by the program; description of government regulatory measures; analysis of social, financial, economic, and other risks associated with the government program, etc.[6] The order On Approving the Methodological Guidelines for the Development and Implementation of Government Programs of Russia does not stipulate the length of each document; depending on the scope and importance of the sector affected, the documents can be quite long.

Government programs are reported on in three stages:

1. *Quarterly Monitoring*: The MoED consistently monitors progress on government programs based on reports provided by the responsible agency. The reporting requirements are prescribed by Order №690, as are the duties of the responsible agency as coordinator of the reporting process. Before the first day of the second month after the quarter, the MoED submits to the government a quarterly progress report for the milestones listed in the implementation plan. Deputy chairmen of the government of Russia coordinate implementation and do a preliminary review of the monitoring outcomes.
2. *Annual Monitoring*: By March 1 of the year following the reporting year, the agencies responsible prepare a progress report on the effectiveness of their government program; a revised annual report must be submitted by May 1. Once prepared, an agency submits its annual report to the government, the MoED, and the MoF and (so long as it does not contain classified and confidential information) posts it on the government programs website. By law the annual report must state:
   - Specific outputs achieved in the reporting period
   - Government program targets (indicators) achieved
   - List of milestones and their achievement, or not—with reasons for not achieving them—by the deadlines in the implementation plan

- List of actions performed or not performed, and reasons for any nonperformance
- Analysis of factors affecting implementation of the government program
- Use of budget appropriations and other sources of funding
- Any amendments the implementing agency has made to the government program
- Analysis of actions affecting priority national projects
- An evaluation of the program's effectiveness
- Proposals for changes to the forms and methods of program management; reduction, increase, or other adjustments to funding; or early termination of key actions or of the entire program.

Within 20 days of receipt of an agency's annual report, the MoED and the MoF must submit their findings to the Government of Russia. If necessary, the government may arrange for a hearing on a progress report prepared by the agency. After review of the report the government may decide to adjust the funding and elements of program design, including specific targets.

3. *Consolidated Annual Report:* The MoED also prepares an annual consolidated progress report on the course of government programs, with an evaluation of their effectiveness, and submits it to the Government of Russia and the MoF by April 1 of the year following the reporting year (a revised report must be submitted by June 1). The report is posted on the government program website based on data from implementing agencies and the MoF on cash expenditures; it contains the following information:
   - Key results for the government programs in the reporting period
   - Consistency of program targets and achievements in the reporting year
   - Expenditure mandates of Russia associated with the programs that have been fulfilled
   - Evaluation of the performance of the responsible agencies as it relates to government programs
   - If needed, proposals on amending methods of managing the government programs, reducing or increasing funding, and on early termination of any actions or the entire program.

The consolidated annual progress report and the program effectiveness evaluation are reviewed at a meeting of the Government of Russia, with special attention to progress reports filed by agencies that were considered ineffective in the previous year. This is a meeting of ministers chaired by the Prime Minister.[7] The ministers report personally on the progress of programs for which their agency is responsible.

Once the government completes the evaluation of the effectiveness of a program, it may decide to cut budget appropriations for the following fiscal year; terminate activities or the entire program early, as of the following fiscal year; or discipline heads of federal executive authorities (for this petitions must be submitted to the President), other chief spending units, and implementing and co-implementing agencies for failure to achieve the targets set for the program. So far, however, there has been little evidence of efforts to systematically target cuts in programs deemed ineffective. Nevertheless, this mechanism is generally considered promising, though its widespread use would be possible only after a significant increase in the quality of government programs, evaluation mechanisms, and experience in conducting programs. Otherwise, there is a high risk of unjustified reallocation of budgeted spending.

Crucially, heads of executive authorities responsible for implementing and participating in government programs bear personal responsibility for the effectiveness of those programs, for falling short of targets or indicators, and for the accuracy of information posted on a program website.

Currently, information on government programs (list of programs, references for enacting government resolutions, key characteristics, volumes of funding, and consolidated annual progress reports) is posted on the official website of the Government of Russia (http://government.ru) and the government program website (http://programs.gov.ru/Portal/). All programs are grouped by subject matter as follows:

1. New quality of life (13 programs)
   a. Health care development
   b. Education development
   c. Social security
   d. Accessible environment
   e. Affordable housing and utilities
   f. Pension system development
   g. Facilitating employment
   h. Rule of law and crime prevention
   i. Prevention of illegal drug trade
   j. Emergency prevention, fire security, and water safety
   k. Promotion of culture and tourism
   l. Environmental control
   m. Promotion of physical culture and sports
2. Innovation and modernization (17 programs)
   a. Developing science and technology
   b. Economic development and innovative economy
   c. Developing industry and its competitiveness
   d. Developing aviation
   e. Developing shipbuilding
   f. Developing the electronic and radio-electronic industry
   g. Developing the pharmaceutical and medical industry
   h. Russia's airspace industry
   i. Developing the nuclear energy sector
   j. Fostering an information society
   k. Developing transport

     l. Developing agriculture
     m. Developing fisheries
     n. Developing foreign economic activities
     o. Rehabilitation and use of natural resources
     p. Developing forestry
     q. Energy efficiency and energy;

3. National security (2 programs)
     a. National defense (classified)
     b. National security (classified)

4. Balanced regional development (6 programs in preparation)
     a. Socioeconomic development of the Far East and the Baikal Region
     b. Developing the Northern Caucasus Federal Region
     c. Promoting federalism and building conditions for effective and accountable regional and local financial management
     d. Socioeconomic development of the Kaliningrad Oblast
     e. Socioeconomic development of Russia's Arctic Zone
     f. Socioeconomic development of the Crimea Federal Okrug

5. Effective government (4 programs)
     a. Federal property management
     b. Public finance management and financial market regulation
     c. Foreign policy
     d. Justice.

In 2015 it was too soon to properly evaluate the quality and effectiveness of government programs. Nevertheless, introduction of program and performance budgeting has triggered a number of important changes in the modus operandi of executive authorities, the quality of their deliverables, the skills of their staff, and their understanding of the situation in their own sector. However, it should be mentioned that the severely inadequate conditions (minimal time to prepare, poor explanations, no training, etc.) that line ministers faced when the government programs were elaborated had some negative effects, such as poor motivation, "new paper burden" attitude, and a lack of comprehensive understanding of the reform targets.

While government programs are a key performance budgeting instrument, they do not embody the very programmatic budgeting concept formulated in the course of reforms. The reason is that according to the Russian legislation, only those expenses captured in the budget law are eligible for funding, and they are based on spending mandates,[8] whereas government programs may envision a broader range of expenditures and bigger outlays. Also, under the current legislation, government programs do not generate expenditure mandates but are merely documents for planning budget appropriations to achieve expected outputs. The point is that incorporating planned spending into a program does not imply an obligation to finance it from the budget. The federal Law on the Federal Budget is the only source of information about real budget expenditures.

The problem is that programs, with their goals and outputs, are not given any priority; they are simply plugged in to the 'old school' system of planning. This is why a comprehensive transition to performance budgeting in Russia requires a move to programmatic budgeting.

The 2012 Program to Enhance the Effectiveness of Budget Expenditures called for amendments to the Budget Code to put in place a legal rationale for moving to programmatic budgeting. However, it was not until 2013 that those amendments were passed; until they were, the term "government program" had not even been mentioned in the Budget Code.

It was in May 2013 that Federal Law №104-FZ *On Amending the Budget Code of the Russian Federation and Certain Regulatory Acts of the Russian Federation Due to Changes in the Budget Code* was adopted. It envisaged changes to the Budget Code to put in place a regulatory framework for government programs (national through municipal) and enable changes in budget classification to align expenditures with planned program outputs and performance indicators. Also envisaged was an annual effectiveness evaluation of every government and municipal program to support decisions about whether a program should be terminated or amended for the following fiscal year. To promote the transparency and accountability of budget appropriations for programs, spending items may be earmarked as in compliance with programs. It could thus be argued that the minimum required legal framework is now in place to apply the programmatic approach across all levels of government and prepare budgets aligned with programs.

Changes in Performance Budgeting over Time

The regulatory foundation for the federal transition to performance budgeting was laid down in 2004. The Concept of the Budget Reform in Russia (the Concept) became the core document underpinning the incipient reform in 2004–06. In essence, the reform called for shifting the focus of the budgeting process from input (resource) management to output management by enhancing the accountability and promoting the independence of budget agents and administrators in light of medium-term targets. The principal goal of the Concept was to create conditions to enable effective management of public and municipal resources. More effective spending was the goal of the reforms, including a transition to performance budgeting.

The "new" budget process was meant to rely on the following critical elements:

- Monitoring expenditure performance
- Shifting to multiyear budget planning
- Changing key targets when forming and adopting the budget by planning expected outputs in terms of the resources required
- Broadening the powers of budget administrators while making them accountable for achieving targeted outputs.

In the course of implementing the Concept, the government of Russia designed new documents that became mandatory for executive authorities. The idea was to clearly highlight planned outputs and the resources needed to achieve them:

- Register of spending mandates
- Reports on outputs and key deliverables
- Targeted programs.

The *Register of Spending Mandates* (2004) became one of the first documents designed to cost out mandates and budget-financed obligations. The original approach assumed that all government authorities would carry out an inventory of their spending mandates in line and quantify the costs of each mandate. However, given the accelerated pace of reform and calls for prompt preparation of the registers, they were generally compiled "backwards"—based on the current budget—with each spending item substantiated by a regulation. But even that approach was useful for systematizing both spending mandates and regulations.

Currently, the registers are compiled by the chief spending units as a list of laws, bylaws, and agreements that give rise to spending mandates, with an estimate of budget appropriations required to fulfill the mandates related to a given program.[9] Registers, which are drawn up for three years, are regularly posted on the MoF website (http://www.minfin.ru/ru/perfomance/reforms/budget/resoriented/registry/).

The *Report on Outcomes and Key Areas of Business* (the Report) was designed as a strategic planning document for the executive authority; it outlines all the goals and objectives of the agency, actions to be implemented, and planned outputs. Regulations related to the Report were adopted along with the Concept and remain in force as amended. Initially, Reports were required to cover the following:

- Goals, objectives, and performance indicators
- Expenditure mandates and revenue sources
- Targeted budget programs and nonprogram activities
- Spending allocations by goals and objectives
- Spending effectiveness.

Reports were expected to list performance indicators for the government authorities. Later, based on reforms already made and the need to shorten Reports (some ran more than 500 pages), a simpler format was authorized. Currently, the Report, which is mandatory for executive authorities, is drafted annually on a rolling three-year basis and published on official websites of executive authorities (e.g., the Report of the MoF of Russia: http://www.minfin.ru/ru/perfomance/reforms/budget/resoriented/report/). Regrettably, this document has never added any real value to the budget process.

Still, it can be thought of as the first shot at a performance budgeting launch, as well as an attempt to formulate agency operational goals and to qualify and quantify agency performance. In practice, it was a challenge for government authorities, who were used to traditional budget management techniques that ignored current circumstances, goals, and objectives, and control over their achievement.

At the outset of the reform, *targeted programs* were the most familiar tool. Launched in 1995, targeted programs were intended to implement the main constitutional guarantees that cover joint jurisdiction by the federal government and the regions—guarantees of education, health care, affordable housing, and agricultural development. Targeted programs are funded through capital spending earmarked for construction or equipment purchases and through R&D spending. In fact, at the time the Concept was adopted, federal programmatic budgeting was carried out in the form of Federal Targeted Programs (FTPs) and Federal Earmarked Investment Programs, though the methodology and implementation were far from perfect.

Resources allocated for most FTPs were a variation of supplementary line-by-line financing to enable the operation of the agencies; the amount of funding changed almost constantly, among other reasons because program goals and output targets were formulated only vaguely. Rather than increasing the number of FTPs or their funding, it was decided to widen their scope by transforming them into Agency Targeted Programs (ATPs) aligned with the standards set for line-by-line spending: clear objectives, measurable outputs, an evaluation framework, and indicators.

In line with this principle, in the Concept FTPs[10] and ATPs[11] were viewed as two types of uniform budget targeted programs that were similar in principle and implementation but differed in substance and status (see table 10.1). An FTP, which is adopted by government decree, is a cross-agency and cross-level program, one that can be implemented by several line ministries and cover both federal and subfederal levels of government; ATPs help organize the activities of their own agencies in a programmatic way and are adopted by order of those agencies.

By the time the reform kicked off, FTPs had been in use for more than 10 years. Nonetheless, their many drawbacks—such as lack of a performance evaluation framework and of structural reform measures, a gap between

Table 10.1 Features of FTPs and ATPs

Parameters	FTP	ATP
Level of approval	Government of the Russian Federation	Executive authority
Nature of the program	Cross-sectoral	Intrasectoral
Substance of program operations and actions	Large-scale in terms of volume and deadlines	Smaller-scale operations, current tasks

planned and actual funding, and poor-quality reports—signaled the need to improve current practice and address those issues. As in the Concept, the response was two-pronged:

- Review the regulatory framework underpinning FTPs to address the issues and transform FTPs into a performance budgeting tool.
- Draft a new document to move the programmatic planning principle from the national level (which addressed systemic cross-sector issues) to the agency level.

ATPs proved to be the answer. It was assumed that the procedures governing ATPs, being smaller in scale, would have simpler design, clearance, and implementation arrangements than FTPs so as to formulate as many programs as possible and move to budget execution based on performance budgeting. However, in practice, federal regulation of the arrangements for ATPs proved to be challenging and complex. Most cumbersome were external appraisal and actual clearance of ATPs by the MoED and the MoF. What complicated matters further was the government's lack of incentives for launching ATPs across the board.

Beginning in 2010, government programs became one of the main instruments for making budget spending more effective. The 2012 Government Program to Enhance the Effectiveness of Budget Expenditures for the first time defined the concept of a government program as a document that (1) detailed the goals, objectives, outputs, and the avenues and tools of government policy to achieve the goals and priorities set by the 2020 Concept for Long-Term Socioeconomic Development of Russia; or (2) enabled large-scale national or international activities. Essentially, government programs were meant to become central to the budget process, aligning federation socioeconomic priorities with budget financing.

The starting point that gave momentum to programmatic budgeting was Government Resolution №588 of August 2, 2010, On *Adopting Regulations for Drafting, Implementing, and Measuring the Effectiveness of Government Programs in the Russian Federation* (Regulations). The Regulations set forth the rules for design, implementation, and measurement of the effectiveness of government programs and for control of their implementation.

Government programs comprise subprograms, which detail ATPs and other activities of government authorities. Subprograms address specific tasks that are part of the programs, their extent depending on the scale and complexity of the area the program addresses.

Until recently, the principles guiding the formulation of government program goals, objectives, and targets were detailed in Methodological Guidelines adopted by the MoED for the design and implementation of government programs in Russia. In 2013 these underwent a major revision—the part of the government program that had to be formally adopted was curtailed, and a requirement was introduced to clear the program with Rosstat, the federal state statistics service—and programs already adopted were then revised.

In 2011, amendments and additions were made to the regulations related to FTPs and ATPs so as to integrate programmatic documents with government programs. New norms stipulated that FTPs and ATPs, already in existence or new, must be incorporated into government programs of Russia—which made and ATPs the new performance budgeting mechanisms. ATPs. being in a sense themselves government programs, had narrower scope, and their role as a structural element of a government program is similar to that of a subprogram.

Also, when the Federal Law on the 2011 Federal Budget and the planned period of 2012 and 2013 was being drafted, for the first time an analytical break-down of expenditures by government programs was made and attached to the law as an appendix.

Thus, as of 2011 the minimum conditions to kick-start design and imple-mentation of government programs in Russia had been put in place. A frame-work had been established to measure the effectiveness of government programs by preparing quarterly and annual reports and consolidated annual reports of how well government programs were progressing. However, since many government programs were not launched until after 2013, the reporting track record is quite short.

Adoption of the Current System

The current performance budgeting framework spans all ministries and agencies, which as expressed in federal regulations and legislation necessitates high-level decision-making. However, the MoF and MoED have been assiduous in laying the groundwork. It was that MoF that initiated budgeting reform generally and wrote the first Concept document. At the same time, the MoED has always been the main agency responsible for appraisal and monitoring FTPs; based on entrenched practices and the previous inter-agency distribution of responsibili-ties, methodologies for the design, approval, and implementation of ATPs have also been delegated to that ministry.

All programs of Russia are subject to approval through government regula-tions, with decisions made at a high political level. This choice was made because, among other reasons, many government programs span large sectors of the economy and are regulated by more than one government authority. Formulation and execution of program-based budgets are governed by the Federation Budget Code, constitutional law in the fiscal area, which prescribes how the budget is to treat government programs. The usefulness and rele-vance of performance budgeting has also been promoted at the highest level, in the annual Budget Addresses of the President of Russia to the Federal Assembly. Reform of the budget process thus enjoys support from the national political leadership and is seen by all executive authorities as a public finance priority.

Performance Information Use

When government programs are drafted, special emphasis is given to identifying quantitative and qualitative performance indicators. As prescribed by law, there are many requirements and restrictions on indicators. For instance:

1. Data on the composition and values of targets (indicators) must be provided according to a prescribed template (table 10.2). The number of targets is determined on the basis of the criteria that are necessary and sufficient to achieve the intended goals and objectives.
2. Targets should be:
   - *Relevant*: The indicator should explicitly capture progress in achieving a goal or delivering on an objective and should cover all the material aspects of achieving the goal or objective.
   - *Accurate*: Errors in measurement should not result in distorted perceptions of government programs, outputs, or outcomes.
   - *Free from bias*: Indicators should deter reporting of misleadingly positive values while actual performance deteriorates; they should create the fewest possible incentives for participants to tamper with the results of government programs.
   - *Comparable*: Indicators should be selected with a view to ensuring continuous accumulation of data and valid comparisons over certain time periods with indicators measuring progress of similar subprograms and similar indicators in other countries.
   - *Unambiguous*: The definition of the indicator should ensure common understanding of the measured feature by both experts and consumers of services; therefore, excessively complicated indicators or those that lack a clear and universally accepted definition or measurement unit should be avoided.
   - *Cost-effective*: Data should be collected at minimum cost; existing data collection procedures should be used as much as possible.
   - *Verifiable*: Primary data collection and processing techniques should allow for validation of data accuracy in an independent monitoring and assessment exercise.

Table 10.2 Template for Reporting on Government Program Targets (Indicators)

№	Target	Measured in:	Values of targets				
			Reporting year	Current year	Next year	First year of the planning period	…..
1.							

Source: MOED Order No. 690 of November 20, 2013, "On Approving the Methodological Guidelines for the Development and Implementation of Government Programs of the Russian Federation."

- *Timely*: Data must be collected regularly with clearly defined frequency and with only a small lag between collection and utilization; for monitoring purposes, data should be reported at least once a year.
3. Government program and subprogram indicators should include indicators that
   - Allow for quantitative measurement of progress toward the program's objectives and goals;
   - Reflect the key parameters of the quality and volume of public service delivery;
   - Capture energy efficiency and saving, labor productivity, and (for sectoral development government programs) creation and upgrading of highly productive and high technology jobs.
4. Government program indicators should be set to measure achievement of goals and delivery on objectives as approved by the President and the Government of Russia in strategic and program documents.
5. Indicators should be assigned quantitative values planned for each year, to be calculated
   - According to methodologies approved by executive authorities and set out in supplementary and supporting documents underlying government programs;
   - According to methodologies approved by international institutions; and
   - On the basis of federal statistical observation.
6. A proposed indicator should give a quantitative measure of the outcomes or outputs of government programs and have a concise and clear name that captures the essence of the phenomenon to be observed.
7. The set of indicators should ensure that attainment of program goals and objectives can be tracked and validated.

Together, all the government programs of Russia contain a wealth of indicators capturing Russia's economic sectors and their development plans (see, for example, annex 10A to this study). The problem is that despite the detailed requirements, in practice the real sets of indicators are far from this perfect image: ministers tend to choose indicators from official state statistics, most of which do not directly describe program output. Line ministries and agencies have the option to collect and compute the indicators themselves when they reflect public opinion as collected in polls and surveys, but their reliability is sometimes questionable. Moreover, separate ministerial statistics would add costs, which would not be acceptable to the MoF.

Indicators are used during the budget planning stage when government agencies submit to the MoF a justification of budget appropriations. This document contains not only the agency's financial plans but also the targets linked to the funds requested. However, the MoF does not have any significant influence on the targets. When the government introduces a federal budget proposal in the legislative assembly, targets are given only in reference, background, and explanatory and supporting documents. The budget proposal, as well as later the budget, does not include actual figures for targets. It thus seems too early to claim that performance budgeting data are fully utilized in budget planning and execution. It is fair to say, then, that use of performance information is quite limited; the line ministers and legislators do not use it in day-to-day mode.

It should be noted, however, that apart from the budget component, all indicators and targets for government programs of Russia are accessible to the public on the official websites of ministries and agencies and on the special website for government programs.

Difficulties with the Current System

Russia's progress so far in implementing performance budgeting is certainly an achievement, but the current system is perceived to have some problems, among them:

- The limited informative value of government program targets; in most cases they do not inform assessment of the real outcomes and are not linked to national strategic goals.
- Imperfect techniques to assess program effectiveness that do not allow meaningful comparisons between programs to inform managerial decision-making.
- Lack of obligation to revisit and adjust programs diagnosed as relatively ineffective at the end of a reporting year, and of rules and procedures for recognizing the results of effectiveness evaluations during budget preparation and when updating longer-term spending projections.
- Low reliability and quality of performance information.
- An excessive paper burden for line ministries that must produce government program documents, the expenditure mandates register, implementation plans, detailed program road maps, agency activity plans, justification of budget appropriations, quarterly and annual reports, etc.

Recent legislative developments, particularly *On Strategic Planning in the Russian Federation*, require a more complete and more clearly defined reflection of policy instruments in government programs, which should enhance their usefulness as strategic planning instruments.

It is important to ensure that government programs are more fully integrated into the budget planning process. Specifically, it is important to describe supplementary budgeting by linking additional appropriations to achievement of program goals and outcomes. Meanwhile, the necessity to perform and deliver under tight fiscal constraints suggests that the administrators of federal budget funds should have more discretion to reallocate funds within programs.

Conclusion

Performance budgeting is still at a formative stage in Russia that involves drafting framework documents, rethinking agency roles in terms of Russia's social and economic development, re-costing spending commitments, compiling a database of targets for analysis, and identifying approaches to evaluating program efficiency and effectiveness. However, some improvements in budgeting can already be reported:

- Periodic assessments and revisions of budget commitments with regard to priority, timeliness, and expedience are now regular practice.
- Authorities have considerably improved their transparency, with all nonclassified data on government programs accessible to the public.
- An extensive database has been compiled and is continuously growing; it offers a wider range of indicators than is provided by official statistics and allows for better analysis of economic issues.
- Approaches are being elaborated to assess government programs comparatively.
- Special emphasis is now given to enhancing the quality of public service delivery, and to public opinion polling.

However, if performance budgeting is to be effective, it will be necessary for Russia to:

- Enhance the credibility of targets and indicators for government programs, and use them more extensively in policy making.
- Fully embrace the program budgeting approach, which is the main objective of the budget reform in Russia.
- Gradually simplify the whole process to make it easier for executive authorities to draft all the necessary documents (government programs, implementation plans, detailed program road maps, agency activity plans, etc.).
- Gradually increase the autonomy, and thus the accountability, of executive authorities to ensure that government programs are conducted efficiently and effectively.
- Intensify the training programs for line ministries to promote the whole reform and also explain the goals of each innovation.

The current performance framework represents considerable progress in Russian budgeting practices in terms of shifting the focus of ministries and agencies from inertial spending of budget funds to planning and achievement of outputs. For the future, priority might be given to more practical application of tools and data sets to better inform political and economic decisions.

Annex 10A: Sample Targets (Indicators) of the Accessible Environment for the 2011–15 Government Program of the Russian Federation

Indicator	Meas-ured in:	Indicator Values					
		2010	2011	2012	2013	2014	2015
Share of priority social, transport, and engineering facilities accessible for the disabled and other groups with limited mobility in the total number of priority facilities	%	12	14.4	16.8	16.8	30.9	45
Share of the disabled who positively assess the accessibility of priority facilities in priority living environments in the total number of surveyed disabled citizens	%	30	31.9	33.7	34.7	44.6	55
Share of the disabled who positively assess the public attitude to disability problems in the total number of surveyed disabled citizens	%	30	32.2	36.6	40.8	45.2	49.6
Share of regional disability examination ("social and medical assessment") offices fitted with special diagnostic equipment in the total number of such offices across the regions	%	10	10	10	15	66	86
Share of the disabled showing positive rehabilitation outcomes in the total number of disabled adults who have received rehabilitation services	%	42.2	42.1	44.4	42.6	43	44
Share of the disabled showing positive rehabilitation outcomes in the total number of disabled children who have received rehabilitation services	%	51.7	54.2	53.4	50.9	51	52

Source: GoR Regulation №297 of April 15, 2014.
Note: Program only, no subprograms.

Notes

1. Executive Order №670 of the MOED of Russia of December 22, 2010 *On Adopting Methodological Guidelines for Design and Implementation of Government Programs in the Russian Federation.*

2. Per MoED Letter №6348-АК/Д19 of April 4, 2011.

3. The procedure for discussions and consultations is very formal, though the public hearings have no significant influence on the program structure. Line ministries make the decisions on goals and objectives, funding levels, and specific actions, which follow the strategic indicators and budget constraints.

4. Government Resolution №588 of August 2, 2010 *On Adopting Regulations on Design, Implementation, and Effectiveness Evaluation of Government Programs in the Russian Federation.*

5. Targeted federal programs focus on particular goals and mostly cover capital and R&D spending. As programmatic instruments, they had existed long before the move to program budgeting began. Therefore, although their efficiency may be questionable, they became part of the government programs, which, in turn, covered whole sectors and both current and capital spending.

6. The complete list of documents is stipulated by MoED Order №690 of November 20, 2013.

7. The details of this procedure are determined by the Rules and Regulations of the Government of the Russian Federation (Government Resolution №260 of June 1, 2004, as later amended).

8. Government Resolution №440 of July 16, 2005, "On the Administration of the Register of Spending Mandates of the Russian Federation."

9. 2005-2014: Government Resolution №440 of July 16, 2005 *On Administering Registers of Expenditure Mandates in the Russian Federation;* as of 2014 - Government Resolution №621 of July 7, 2014 *On Administering Registers of Expenditure Mandates in the Russian Federation.*

10. The rules for design and implementation of FTPs were first adopted in 1995 by Government Resolution №.594.

11. Government Resolution №239 of April 19, 2005, adopted regulations on design, adoption, and implementation of ATPs.

CHAPTER 11

United States

Donald Moynihan

Introduction

This book reviews the experience of the U.S. federal government with performance budgeting. Although the United States has tried a variety of different performance systems over the past 20 years, it still struggles with many of the same basic problems with performance budgeting as do other countries—notably a general reluctance of the legislative branch to pay attention to performance data when it makes budget decisions. The decentralized nature of the federal system also adds a layer of complexity to performance budgeting efforts. Nevertheless, the system has evolved. The most recent iteration has emphasized creating routines in the executive branch to foster the use of performance data to generate organizational learning.

Performance Budgeting in the United States

The current U.S. performance system is defined by the GPRA Modernization Act of 2010, the third performance budgeting initiative in the past 20 years (see table 11.1).[1] Later sections will describe continuity and change between these systems, and the motivation for these choices. The Modernization Act updated the Government Performance and Results Act (GPRA) of 1993. GPRA had required, for the first time, that each agency complete strategic plans, measure performance annually, and make the results public.

Because it believed that GPRA was having little impact, the George W. Bush administration added a new performance system: The Program Assessment Rating Tool (PART) was a questionnaire that sought to assess the quality of every government program, grading more than 1,000 programs between 2002 and 2008. First, agency employees filled in the PART assessment and then officials of the Office of Management and Budget (OMB, the central budget authority) reviewed their answers and made final determinations as to the appropriate response. Each program was assigned a score that converted to an evaluation of effective, moderately effective, adequate, ineffective, or results not demonstrated, on the basis of four criteria: program purpose and design, strategic planning,

Table 11.1 Performance Systems for the U.S. Federal Government

Law	Requirements
Government Performance and Results Act (GPRA) 1993–2010	Agencies are required to provide • Five-year strategic plans • Annual performance reports • Annual performance plans
Program Assessment Rating Tool (PART) 2002–2008	• Questionnaire and evaluation applied to each government program • Programs graded on purpose and design, strategic planning, management, and results • Programs ranked from "ineffective" to "effective"
GPRA Modernization Act 2010–current	• Act retains GPRA strategic plans and performance reports. • Agency leaders commit to achieving high-priority goals. • Agencies work together on cross-agency priorities. • Significant goals are reported and reviewed by officials each quarter and each is assigned a specific goal leader. • Each agency has a chief operating officer and a performance improvement officer. • A centralized government website tracks performance information (www.performance.gov). • OMB reviews agency performance and can take remedial action if goals are missed.

program management, and program results/accountability (see Moynihan 2008 for a detailed description of PART). These evaluations accompanied the president's budget proposals to Congress. PART was discontinued with the arrival of the Obama administration in 2009.

The Modernization Act retained or only slightly modified some basic aspects of GPRA. Strategic planning requirements remain but now have a four-year time frame to align with the presidential election calendar. Agencies[2] must continue to complete annual performance plans and reports. There is a greater expectation that targets identified in the performance plan will be aligned with goals in strategic plans. When reporting actual results, agencies are asked to compare results not only with targets but also with at least two years of previous results if available (longer if appropriate), and they must explain progress on goals.

A new requirement in the Modernization Act is that agencies designate a small number (no more than five) agency priority goals. These are targets for which the head of the agency commits to seek improvement within two years; they must be updated quarterly. In addition to identifying these goals, agencies are still expected to track the performance of programs whose goals are not formally defined as agency priorities.

The Modernization Act recognizes that many important government goals are the responsibility of more than one agency. It requires OMB to produce a federal government performance plan featuring cross-cutting priority goals, which OMB calls cross-agency priority goals. In turn, agency plans need to identify how they contribute to these goals. The goals must be reviewed quarterly by OMB staff, and each is assigned a goal leader (in practice this has often been a White House official sharing duties with an agency representative). OMB staff are directed to ensure that different agencies use common indicators that contribute to cross agency priority goals and identify management problems that might undermine the goals. The goals are intended to be few in number and long-term in nature (revised or updated every four years); they are a mixture of explicit policy objectives and management-focused changes.

For the first time, there is a central government website, www.performance .gov, that tracks major goals and links to agency strategic and performance plans. Previously, although agencies were expected to make such plans public, it was not always easy to find them. The new website makes performance information easier to access.

The Modernization Act also establishes new performance management roles. Each agency must have a chief operating officer (COO) and a performance improvement officer (PIO) to oversee performance improvement efforts. The act establishes a governmentwide Performance Improvement Council, made up of the OMB deputy director for management and agency PIOs. The council is expected to share lessons and offer operational advice on implementing performance management practices.

Another significant aspect of the Modernization Act is that it requires formal routines for agency staff to discuss data. Agencies must hold quarterly reviews (sometimes called data-driven reviews) of progress on agency priorities and other significant goals. The COO is required to lead these reviews, and there is detailed discussion of progress on each goal by senior managers and the designated goal leader. The goal leader must track performance outcomes, understand why they rise and fall, and organize efforts for improvement. On www.performance.gov goal leaders are identified—with pictures—alongside the goals they oversee. Table 11.2 sets out the guidance that OMB provides to agencies on how

Table 11.2 Guidance to Agencies for Quarterly Reviews

- Review with the appropriate goal leader the progress achieved during the most recent quarter, overall trend data, and the likelihood of meeting the planned level of performance.
- Hold goal leaders accountable for knowing whether or not their performance indicators are trending in the right direction at a reasonable speed, and if they are not, for understanding why they are not and for having a plan to accelerate progress to the goal.
- Hold goal leaders accountable for knowing the quality of their data, for having a plan to improve it if necessary, and for filling critical evidence or other information gaps.
- Hold goal leaders accountable for identifying effective practices by searching the literature, looking for benchmarks, and analyzing disaggregated data to find positive outliers among performance units.
- Hold goal leaders accountable for validating promising practices with replication demonstrations or other evidence-based methods.
- Review variations in performance trends across the organization and delivery partners, identify possible reasons for each variance, and understand whether the variance points to promising practices or problems needing more attention.
- Include evaluation staff to share and review performance information and evaluation findings; better understand performance issues that evaluation and research studies can help to address; and refine performance measures and indicators.

table continues next page

Toward Next-Generation Performance Budgeting • http://dx.doi.org/10.1596/978-1-4648-0954-5

Table 11.2 Guidance to Agencies for Quarterly Reviews *(continued)*

- Include, as appropriate, relevant personnel within and outside the agency who contribute to the accomplishment of each Agency Priority Goal (or other priority).
- Support the goal leaders in assuring other organizations and programs are contributing as expected to Agency Priority Goals (or other priorities).
- Identify Agency Priority Goals (or other priorities) at risk of not achieving the planned level of performance and work with goal leaders to identify strategies that support performance improvement.
- Encourage a meaningful dialogue around what works, what does not, and the best way to move forward on the organization's top priorities, using a variety of appropriate analytical and evaluation methods.
- Establish an environment that promotes learning and sharing openly about successes and challenges.
- Agree on follow-up actions at each meeting and track timely follow-through.

Source: OMB Circular A-11, 2013a.

quarterly reviews should work and the role of the goal leader. As is clear, goal leaders are not only accountable for the actual performance of an outcome but are expected to both demonstrate knowledge of how it is progressing and offer ideas for improvements. The Modernization Act does not have pay-for-performance provisions, and there are no performance-based contracts or pay incentives for goal leaders. However, the visibility of their association with a goal, and the specific roles they must fill in the quarterly reviews provides an incentive to develop expertise and an agenda for improving outcomes.

The Modernization Act directs OMB to annually identify goals agencies have failed to achieve and require remedial action. Interpreting this provision more broadly than authorizing punishment, OMB has sought to turn it into an opportunity to provide strategic guidance. About 300 of the most prominent agency goals are to be subject to these reviews, which the OMB has named Strategic Objectives Annual Review (SOAR).[3]

How Is Performance Budgeting Defined?

The Modernization Act does not explicitly present itself as a performance budgeting framework—a nod to institutional realities and past experience. Both GPRA and PART laid out an explicit goal of connecting performance data to the budget process. The cumulative evidence (described in the following *Use of Performance Information* section) suggests that neither reform had a systematic effect on resource allocation decisions. This partly reflects the structure of the U.S. system of government. Final budget authority rests with Congress, not the White House. Even though Congress passed both GPRA and the Modernization Act, it has historically resisted performance systems, which are perceived as curbing its discretion.

Compared to GPRA and PART, the Modernization Act downplayed the possibility of performance budgeting. Indeed, there is no mention of the term in the act; nor did the act create processes with the primary purpose of more closely integrating budgets and performance information. Instead of calling for performance budgeting, the Obama administration has instead framed the goal of the Modernization Act as being to more generally encourage use of performance information, arguing that the "ultimate test of an effective performance management system is whether it is used, not the number of goals and measures produced" (OMB 2011, 73). The White House proposed to use performance information not specifically for budgeting purposes but "to lead, learn, and improve outcomes." The Senate report on the Modernization Act similarly offers the view that the act is "aimed at increasing the use of performance information to improve performance and results" (U.S. Senate Committee and Governmental Affairs 2010, 11–12).

Rather than building a system that assumes that Congress will use performance data, the Modernization Act instead targets agency managers, with performance improvement coming via organizational learning. At the same time, agencies must continue to provide performance information as part of their budget submission. In its guidance for this process, the OMB suggests that performance-informed budgeting might be possible, cautioning that performance data are just one factor in the decision process. "Performance information in the Annual Performance Plan, especially the goals, indicators of past performance and other evidence such as evaluations, should inform agency budget decisions, complementing other factors considered in the budget process" (OMB 2013a, 240–42).

Links with Other Forms of Budget Analysis

Program Budgets: Performance data must accompany the budget. The measures are expected to roughly align with program activities, though agencies are given some leeway in how they are presented. During the Bush administration, OMB directed agencies to organize budgets around performance goals. When agencies sent these budgets to Congress, they were actively resisted (Moynihan 2008). Some congressional committees told departments to publish the performance budgets in a section separate from the traditional budget format so they could be more easily ignored. Some committees went further, warning departments not to send performance budgets at all. As a result, the Obama administration allows agencies to structure their budget submission around performance goals if Congressional appropriations committees are open to such an approach, but does not require it.

Program Evaluation: Agencies have historically undertaken evaluations of their programs, though evaluation capacity varies a good deal by agency. Agencies rarely complete evaluations themselves but contract with private companies or universities to do so.

Historically, agency staff who oversaw evaluations were different from the staff responsible for performance data and did not interact with them much. During the Bush administration, PART required agencies to present both performance data and evaluations to be considered when agencies were judged on their effectiveness—a relatively rare effort to integrate the two types of evidence. Under Obama, integration continues, with OMB (2013a, 2013b) directing agencies to:

- Rely on both evaluations and performance data in presenting evidence of goals;
- Include program evaluation staff and evidence in quarterly reviews (see table 11.2); and
- Identify where additional evaluations are needed to assess program effectiveness in strategic reviews with OMB.

OMB has also encouraged agencies to incorporate evaluations into federally funded grants to state and local governments by tying the grants to the amount of evidence supporting the grant proposal. This has been characterized as a "tiered" approach to linking evidence and grants: initiatives that have solid evidentiary support can apply for funds to scale up and receive the maximum funding, initiatives that have some support receive less funding but can seek evaluation support, and those not supported by evidence receive the least funding. These criteria have not yet reshaped the majority of grant funding; just five agencies have proposed grant programs using these criteria (OMB 2013b).

The Department of Education is a leading example of the effort to use evaluations to inform funding decisions. It has a "what works" clearinghouse that reviews evaluations of educational interventions, giving policymakers and educators information on which practices have the strongest evidentiary support.[4] The Obama administration also used stimulus money to create an Investing in Innovation fund that has applied the same tiered logic to supporting grants to states. Indeed, one of the department's performance goals is to increase the percentage of grant dollars that reward the use of evidence.

Changes in Performance Budgeting over Time

The U.S. case illustrates not only the episodic nature of performance budgeting reforms but also the potential for these reforms to evolve. While GPRA marks the beginning of the most recent chapter of performance budgeting, it has a longer history. Indeed, as far back as the 1950 Budgeting and Accounting Procedures Act, agencies were required to formulate budgets around "functions and activities" they intended to achieve.

Historically, the episodic character of federal efforts to institute forms of performance budgeting was largely due to the tendency of new presidents to discard the initiatives of their predecessors. President Nixon eliminated the Planning-Programming-Budgeting System, which was created under President Kennedy and expanded during the Johnson administration,[5] and replaced it with a version of management-by-objectives. In turn, President Carter replaced management by objectives with a new initiative, zero-based budgeting, which was then abandoned by the Reagan administration. The inconstancy of these initiatives encouraged cynicism among the federal employees who were expected to implement them.

By contrast, the last two decades, featuring the Clinton, Bush, and Obama administrations, have seen a gradual evolution of the federal system. Lessons seem to have been learned about the prospects and limitations of performance budgeting in the particular context of the U.S. system of government.

What lessons have emerged from this process?

The first is to *refine expectations about the potential of performance budgeting*. The authors of the Modernization Act and the Obama administration chose not to frame the system as a form of performance budgeting after the perceived failure of the Bush administration in this area and recognized the reality that while Congress had passed the new performance system, that did not mean legislators were likely to use performance data to influence budget decisions. The more realistic goal reflected in the Modernization Act is performance-*informed* budgeting, which recognizes that the greatest benefit of performance techniques in the U.S. setting was in management, not budgeting. The significant reforms in the Modernization Act (goal leaders, quarterly reviews, cross-agency goals, agency priority goals, requiring COOs and PIOs) were all directed to reshaping the organizational environment within the executive branch, rather than creating a performance budgeting system.

A second lesson that flows from the first is to *build routines for performance information use*. Over time policymakers had become aware that the existing performance system had generated a good deal of information, but it was not being widely used. The changes in the Modernization Act were explicitly designed to facilitate the use of performance data.

The original GPRA had put in place organizational routines to measure and disseminate data. With quarterly performance reviews, the Modernization Act instituted new routines that required regular use, or at least discussion, of performance information. The quarterly reviews borrowed an idea that some state and local governments, and even some federal agencies, had already adopted, which was to have regular data-driven reviews of performance. The best-known examples of these reviews were Compstat, a review of policing metrics in New York City, and Citistat in the City of Baltimore (Behn 2007). These meetings featured detailed reviews of performance data, identifying outliers and problem areas, discussing and implementing potential solutions, and reporting on their effects at future meetings.

Another lesson in the evolution of the U.S. performance system is the need to *build agency leadership buy-in*. One of the clearest research findings about performance management is that such systems are more likely to succeed when agency leaders are seen to be committed to the performance system, or to results in general (Gilmour 2006; Moynihan 2008; Dull 2009; Moynihan and Lavertu 2012). In the U.S. system, these leaders are political appointees rather than career officials and may have little experience of or inclination for management. New policy proposals and unanticipated events will always demand their time and attention, which may come at the expense of performance issues.

The requirements of the Modernization Act are intended to discipline agency leaders to set aside the time to think systematically about improving both existing goals and strategic choices for the future. One critique of both PART and GPRA is that they generated so much information that it was impossible for a leader to keep track of what was important. The new visibility, limited number, and short-term nature of high-priority goals are intended to make performance goals more tangible. The 24-month time frame associated with agency priority goals is designed to reflect the relatively short time in office of the average political appointee.

By publicly linking agency leaders and goal leaders to goal achievement, reformers hope to draw upon the desire of individuals to protect their reputation. This can be a powerful motivator, especially in systems like the U.S. where there is high turnover among senior leaders over time, and success in one job paves the way for the next one.

The Modernization Act also seeks to ensure that there is a team around agency leaders to support performance. Here, the Modernization Act drew upon Bush administration initiatives. The Bush administration created the positions of PIO and COO for each agency by executive order and established the Performance Improvement Council. The Obama administration kept this executive order in place, and the Modernization Act embedded it in statute.

Adoption of the Current System

The passage of the Modernization Act, which was not a high-profile political battle, did not receive a great deal of attention. In one respect, its adoption was remarkable because it came at a time when deep partisan disagreement between the primary political parties had stymied most significant policy changes.

The original GPRA was a product of Congress; although President Clinton supported it, the idea emerged from Congress. The Modernization Act benefited from the perception that it only slightly modified existing law and updated a tool that Congress had designed to exercise oversight over the executive branch. By contrast, Congress had chosen not to adopt PART as a permanent process, partly because it was closely identified with President Bush and seen as an exercise in executive power.

Even if PART was not retained, its use during the Bush years still had value in propelling passage of the Modernization Act, since it created a sense that GPRA was not sufficient and something new was required. For a number of years a Representative from Texas, Henry Cuellar, had proposed revising GPRA, and in 2010 his efforts gained support from Senators Mark Warner (VA) and Tom Carper (DE). The Modernization Act was not a prominent political issue at a time when President Obama and Republicans in Congress were at loggerheads and was not closely identified with the president; its low profile may have smoothed its passage. The final version of the law passed in the House of Representatives largely on the basis of support from Democrats and passed with little disagreement in the Senate at a time when more widely debated policy issues were stuck in partisan deadlock.

As a candidate, Obama had spoken generally about a pragmatic and results-oriented approach to government in ways that were similar to the emphasis President Bush had given the topic. While the president did not actively lobby for or discuss the Modernization Act, many of the ideas it featured had been promoted by his political appointees at OMB (Metzenbaum 2009; Zients 2009) and were already being put in place before the statute required. There was, therefore, a sense that OMB cared about the Modernization Act and would work aggressively to facilitate its success. Indeed, OMB is the law's most important stakeholder; although Congress passed the Modernization Act, with requirements for congressional consultation on strategic planning, it has not shown great interest in using it.

Performance Information Use

Governmentwide Use

A basic way to assess the effectiveness of performance systems is whether data are actually being used. Both GPRA and PART had an explicit goal of connecting performance data to the budget process, but there is little evidence that either reform had much effect on resource decisions. There is neither substantial data nor anecdotal evidence that GPRA had much effect (Radin 2006), and the Bush administration put PART in place partly because of a perception that GPRA had failed, saying "After eight years of experience [since the creation of GPRA], progress toward the use of performance information for program management has been discouraging" (OMB 2001, 27).

There was more systematic evidence for PART. Its use of summary program effectiveness scores allowed researchers to examine whether incremental changes in budget allocations were correlated with these scores. Some initial evidence suggested this was happening, at least within the executive branch. In the president's budget proposals to Congress, justifications to cut programs would sometimes refer to PART (Moynihan 2008), and one study found a modest correlation between PART scores and proposed budget changes (Gilmour and Lewis 2006). This fits with qualitative accounts of OMB staff taking PART seriously, using it as at least one relevant piece of information in budget decisions (Moynihan 2008; Posner and Fantone 2007). It also makes a good deal of sense that OMB officials might be at least somewhat likely to pay attention to the results of the tool they had developed.

But because actual budget appropriations are determined by Congress, not the president, it is more important to understand how PART was received by the legislative branch. Here, researchers have generally found that PART did not have an effect on appropriations, congressional actors paid little attention to it (Redburn and Newcomer 2008), and PART scores did not systematically influence budget decisions. Efforts by the Bush administration to design budget submissions around program objectives were rebuffed by Congressional budget officials, who consistently told agencies they disliked any change in the format of the budget data they received (Moynihan 2008). Content analyses of congressional budget deliberations suggested that PART was not widely used, and it even appeared that it lost influence over time (Frisco and Stalebrink 2008). One reason for this resistance is that congressional staffers often doubted the conclusions that less-experienced OMB staff drew from PART (White 2012). Heinrich (2012) offered the most careful attempt to link PART to congressional decisions, but in examining 95 Health and Human Service programs, she found no connection between PART scores and budget changes.

There have been no careful studies of whether budgeting staff at OMB or in Congress are using performance data more since passage of the Modernization Act. At a macro level, debates over budgets have been marked by partisan showdowns between President Obama and the Republican Party, leading to a government shutdown and automated across-the-board cuts (a process known as sequestration). Such instability provides little room for careful analysis of program performance, though it may be that data are being used at a more micro level, in agency and OMB choices about proposed budget levels and by legislative staff about specific programs.

Performance budgeting can occur not just in budget allocation decisions but also in how managers make decisions, including resource decisions. The Government Accountability Office (GAO) has regularly surveyed federal managers on whether they use performance data in making a range of decisions. Based on these surveys, one study suggested that GPRA and PART did little to facilitate the use of performance data to making such decisions as setting program priorities, changing processes, allocating resources, taking action to correct program problems, setting employee job expectations, and rewarding employees (Moynihan and Lavertu 2012). However, managers who have been exposed to the routines created by the Modernization Act—data-driven meetings, creating cross-agency goals and agency priority goals—were more likely to say that they used performance data to make managerial and resource allocation decisions (Moynihan and Kroll 2016).

In short, there is little evidence that GPRA and PART facilitated much more than a presentational form of performance budgeting, though there is some evidence that the Modernization Act is encouraging a performance-informed approach, at least for managers in the executive branch. The results make sense if it is assumed that performance systems create routines that encourage certain types of behaviors. GPRA and PART routines centered on measuring and disseminating data. These routines are observable—elected officials and OMB can tell if they have been completed—but they are not the same as actual use of the data. Agencies must comply with these requirements, but their employees have discretion about whether to use the information that emerges. This creates an incentive for passive response. For the Modernization Act, the required routines, which are more centered on data use, appear to have had some success.

Difficulties with the Performance System

Political Support

The U.S. has had difficulties with its performance system. Perhaps the most fundamental is the relative lack of interest Congress has shown in using performance data. Performance initiatives generally enjoy broad, but not deep, political support. While in some situations having a political champion is an advantage, the partisanship that currently characterizes the U.S. system means that reforms closely identified with a particular president (as PART was with President Bush) may actually generate political opposition and distrust.

Because the performance system is now entrenched in the law, it cannot be easily abandoned, and it is not likely to be changed any time soon. Political support will matter for how vigorously the next president will implement the Modernization Act. However, as long as senior officials at OMB and the GAO continue to treat performance as a priority, the Modernization Act will have enough impetus to continue.

Capacity and Resources

One of the difficulties with performance budgeting over the last 20 years is that few extra resources were provided to manage the transaction costs of collecting and disseminating data. This responsibility was generally left to budget staff in agencies, which helps to explain the passive response to GPRA and PART—their requirements, piled on top of existing responsibilities, were seen as secondary to employees' primary responsibilities. The Bush administration's creation of the positions of COOs and PIOs was a belated acknowledgement that specialized staff were needed to take charge of the performance system.

When GPRA was first operational, there was an attempt to train staff in the basics of strategic planning and performance measurement, but resources for training have eroded during the last decade, and this mechanism to build awareness and capacity for performance budgeting has been underutilized. The Modernization Act directed the Office of Personnel Management (OPM) to identify the personnel skills needed to engage with the Modernization Act and to lead training in this area. Though some progress has been made, training remains under-resourced because of the general budget constraints. OPM has also drawn up job descriptions that explicitly mention the performance analysis skills new employees need.

The Trustworthiness of Data

The institutional design of the U.S. government creates natural tensions between the executive and legislative branches, and the heightened partisanship between Democrats and Republicans exacerbates the potential for legislative mistrust of data generated by the executive branch. These tensions were most apparent during the Bush administration, where Democrats argued that PART was being used by the White House to attack liberal programs. While OMB had sought to make PART politically neutral, later analyses revealed that programs housed in departments viewed as more liberal (e.g., environmental and welfare departments) were given systematically lower scores than other departments (Gallo and Lewis 2012). This mistrust of PART appeared to extend to how federal employees responded to it—employees in more liberal agencies were less likely than peers in conservative agencies to use performance data if exposed to PART (Lavertu and Moynihan 2012), and they reported PART assessments as being more burdensome (Lavertu, Lewis, and Moynihan 2013).

The legislative origins of the Modernization Act should reduce some of that distrust, and Congress can turn to the GAO to audit agency performance processes if they are concerned about data quality. However, evidence of systematic data manipulation in medical appointment wait times for military veterans in 2014 (detailed in the following section) has raised skepticism about performance data.

Lack of Broader Change
In the United States the introduction of performance reforms was for the most part not associated with broader organizational change for core employees. The traditional civil service constraints and protections remained, though there are some exceptions. When the enormous new Department of Homeland Security was created in 2002, President Bush sought to exempt its employees from traditional civil service rules, but public sector unions appealed and most traditional rules were reinstituted by the courts.

The decentralization of the U.S. system has allowed for increasing managerial flexibility in a number of policy areas, compounded by the gradual trend toward use of private contractors for many services. In the area of education, new performance standards have been accompanied by frequently acrimonious political battles that in many states have weakened teacher job security.

Debates about broad rule changes are highly partisan, with Republicans arguing for privatization and reducing protections for public employees, and Democrats, who rely on public sector unions for support, generally opposing such changes. The partisan framing of these discussions has weakened the capacity to build agreement on broad public sector changes, or to connect such changes to performance budgeting practices.

Cross-Cutting Goals and Fragmented Governance
The Modernization Act seeks to deal with the complexity of tying performance measures to tasks that cut across the responsibility of multiple agencies by establishing cross-agency priority goals. Agencies must now identify how they contribute to such goals, and OMB is charged with ensuring that agencies use the same metrics.

The federalist design of the U.S. government makes applying performance measures more complex in another dimension. Relatively few services to citizens are provided directly by federal employees; federal funding of services by others is more common, with the actual services being provided by state and local governments and increasingly by private entities. These relationships are usually not directly structured through performance contracts, although there may sometimes be incentives for performance that align with the president's policy goals. For example, states were offered performance bonuses for reducing the number of welfare seekers under Presidents Bush and Clinton, and President Obama offered incentives to make it easier for children in poor families to access public health insurance. Critics also argue that the imperative to have a single set of federal measures discourages innovation by state governments and instead encourages a one-size-fits-all approach (Radin 2006) or use of state-to-state performance indicators that are only superficially comparable, as was the case with the No Child Left Behind (NCLB) act (Davidson et al. 2013). A related concern is that the federal government has limited capacity to monitor the reliability of performance data produced by local governments, states, or other providers, especially private ones (Soss, Fording, and Schram 2011).

Misuse of Performance Data

There has been evidence of perverse responses to performance budgeting in a variety of policy areas, and in recent years the evidence has become more public, increasing concern about problems with performance measurement systems in specific policy areas.

Education is the most prominent policy area and the longest-lasting concern. Critics have argued that NCLB and Race to the Top have encouraged teaching to the test rather than developing broader education or analytical skills. There has also been evidence of outright cheating. Analysis of test scores in Chicago, for instance, showed that teachers had tampered with tests (Jacob and Levitt 2003). Such problems became more public after a criminal investigation in the City of Atlanta uncovered evidence of teachers systematically altering test results. Senior leaders in the school district had gained national praise for the apparent improvement in student outcomes, but investigations revealed an organizational culture where failing to improve scores was not accepted, and where concerns about cheating were ignored (Winerip 2013).

Research on publicly funded job training programs for welfare recipients has also shown that performance incentives have often led to perverse behavior, with caseworkers focusing on short-term placement rather than job quality, ignoring or systematically excluding hard-to-place clients, and manipulating the data they reported to higher levels of government (Heinrich 2007; Heinrich and Marschke 2010; Soss, Fording, and Schram 2011).

In 2014 controversy arose about the health care services provided to military veterans by the Veterans Health Administration. In this case, the providers were federal employees, and the organization had traditionally enjoyed a positive reputation. The parent department, Veterans Affairs, was led by a well-regarded former general, Eric Shinseki, who could point to performance improvements in reducing the risk of homelessness of former veterans. However, an internal audit confirmed accusations that officials at the Veterans Health Administration were systematically manipulating appointment dates to disguise long backlogs. Senior managers in the health system had performance incentives tied to, among other things, meeting a 14-day window to give clients appointments. As a result, Shinseki resigned, and criminal investigations are taking place. This marks the first time a senior U.S. federal official lost his position due to failures tied to performance measures, and the resulting lesson may be that scandals related to data manipulation are more costly than actual performance improvements are beneficial.

The Modernization Act itself did not link goal achievement to pay, or to harsh penalties. Not only would that have made for a more contentious passage of the law, it also reflects concerns about the limits of extrinsic rewards for tasks that may be complex, hard to measure, and multi-dimensional. In those conditions, pay systems would be tied to measures that do not fully capture performance— and may encourage perverse behavior. However, with the use of performance incentives in grants, contracts with private providers, and even within the pay system for many federal employees, there are still opportunities for extrinsic incentives.

Conclusion

The current state of performance budgeting in the United States might be described as a wary but pragmatic optimism. The experiences of GPRA and PART have made officials cautious about the limits of performance budgeting— it has become rare to find a public official who will argue that performance data should, or even can, drive budget decisions. Performance-informed budgeting is offered as a more realistic aspiration, and even then, the dominance of Congress in setting budgets, and its traditional lack of interest in performance data, limits the potential for a closer link between data and budgeting. That is one fundamental difference between the U.S. and parliamentary systems, where finance ministries can shape the final budget.

At the same time, there has been a sustained effort to work within these constraints by embedding consideration of performance data into how public entities operate. Key provisions of the Modernization Act seek to change the basic structure of organizational routines for executive branch officials, requiring them to consider performance data more frequently and to make public commitments to pursue performance goals. Better integrating performance data with evaluations offers the potential for a richer understanding of performance than occurs when only performance data are considered. For other countries looking at the U.S. system for ideas on how to better use performance data, these aspects of the Modernization Act offer the most promise.

The fact that the U.S. has a federal system is another consideration when this case is compared with others. Arguably, that makes it harder to use performance budgeting at the federal level, since federal officials do not directly control many services. But the example of education demonstrates that federal officials may still have a very powerful role in encouraging attention to performance at lower levels of government.

It is worth speculating about how the performance system in the U.S. was able to evolve over the last 20 years, especially given the tradition of presidents abandoning the reforms of their predecessors. Progress may at times seem slow and unsteady, but the federal government has captured, stored, and disseminated lessons on how to upgrade the performance system, learning from past mistakes and experimenting with new approaches. Embedding the performance system in statutes has restricted presidents from making dramatic changes and ensured that the changes put in place with the Modernization Act have broad support. The U.S. has also benefited from continuing interest in the topic. A community of government officials, especially in the GAO and OMB, and outside observers from think tanks and academia have continually engaged in a dialogue, allowing for the emergence of a consensus about problems with the performance system, which ones are fixable, and how to fix them. These lessons have been incremental in that they adapted an existing system and were informed by experience at the federal level itself, rather than adapting an entire system from elsewhere. As a result, the system that has evolved matches the possibilities and limitations of the setting in which it occurs.

Notes

1. The text of the Modernization Act can be found at http://www.gpo.gov/fdsys/pkg /PLAW-111publ352/pdf/PLAW-111publ352.pdf. Agencies receive specific guidance on how to complete the requirements of the act from OMB budget instructions, specifically part 6 of Circular A-11, which is published at http://www.whitehouse .gov/omb/circulars_a11_current_year_a11_toc.

2. In the U.S., "agency" is used more broadly than in most other countries to categorize any stand-alone government entity. The requirements of the Modernization Act apply to all executive departments, government corporations, and independent establishments. They do not apply to the Central Intelligence Agency, the Government Accountability Office, the Panama Canal Commission, the United States Postal Service, and the Postal Regulatory Commission.

3. OMB Guidance on SOAR can be found at http://www.whitehouse.gov/sites/default /files/omb/assets/a11_current_year/s270.pdf.

4. The clearinghouse can be found at http://ies.ed.gov/ncee/wwc/.

5. The system was retained in a modified form in the Department of Defense. For a more detailed history of federal performance budgeting efforts before GPRA, see GAO 1997.

Bibliography

Behn, Robert. 2007. *What All Mayors Would Like to Know about Baltimore's CitiState Performance Strategy*. Washington, DC: IBM Center for the Business of Government.

Davidson, Elizabeth, Randall Reback, Jonah Rocko, and Heather L. Schwartz. 2013. "Fifty Ways to Leave a Child Behind: Idiosyncrasies and Discrepancies in States' implementation of NCLB." Working paper, National Bureau of Economic Research, Cambridge, MA. http://www.nber.org/papers/w18988.pdf.

Dull, Matthew. 2009. "Results-model Reform Leadership: Questions of Credible Commitment". *Journal of Public Administration Research and Theory* 19 (2): 255–84.

Frisco, Velda, and Odd Stalebrink. 2008. "Congressional Use of the Program Assessment Rating Tool." *Public Budgeting and Finance* 28 (2): 1–19.

Gallo, Nick, and David E. Lewis. 2012. "The Consequences of Presidential Patronage for Federal Agency Performance." *Journal of Public Administration Research and Theory* 22 (2): 195–217.

Gilmour, John B. 2006. *Implementing OMB's Program Assessment Rating Tool (PART): Meeting the Challenges of Integrating Budget and Performance*. Washington, DC: IBM Center for the Business of Government.

Gilmour, John B., and David E. Lewis. 2006. "Assessing Performance Budgeting at OMB: The Influence of Politics, Performance, and Program Size." *Journal of Public Administration Research and Theory* 16: 169–86.

Government Accountability Office. 1997. *Performance Budgeting: Past Initiatives Offer Insights into GPRA Implementation*. Washington, DC: GAO.

Hatry, Harry P. 2007. *Performance Measurement: Getting Results*. 2nd ed. Washington, DC: Urban Institute.

Heinrich, Carolyn. 2007. "False or Fitting Recognition: The Use of High Performance Bonuses in Motivating Organizational Achievements." *Journal of Policy Analysis and Management* 26 (2): 281–304.

———. 2012. "How Credible Is the Evidence, and Does It Matter? An Analysis of the Program Assessment Rating Tool." *Public Administration Review* 72 (1): 123–34.

Heinrich, Carolyn H., and Gerald Marschke. 2010. "Incentives and Their Dynamics in Public Sector Performance Management Systems." *Journal of Policy Analysis and Management* 29 (1): 183–208.

Jacob, Brian A., and Steven Levitt. 2003. "Rotten Apples: An Investigation of the Prevalence and Predictors of Teacher Cheating." *Quarterly Journal of Economics* 118 (3): 843–77.

Joyce, Philip G. 2011. "The Obama Administration and PBB: Building on the Legacy of Federal Performance-informed Budgeting." *Public Administration Review* 71 (3): 356–67.

Lavertu, Stéphane, David Lewis, and Donald Moynihan. 2013. "Administrative Reform, Ideology and Bureaucratic Effort: Performance Management in the Bush Era." *Public Administration Review* 73 (6): 845–57.

Lavertu, Stéphane, and Donald P. Moynihan. 2013. "Agency Political Ideology and Reform Implementation: Performance Management in the Bush Administration." *Journal of Public Administration Research and Theory* 23 (3): 521–49.

Metzenbaum, Shelley. 2009. *Performance Management Recommendations for the New Administration*. Washington, DC: IBM Center for the Business of Government.

Moynihan, Donald. 2008. *The Dynamics of Performance Management: Constructing Information and Reform*. Washington, DC: Georgetown University Press.

———. 2013a. "Advancing the Empirical Study of Performance Management What We Learned from the Program Assessment Rating Tool." *American Review of Public Administration* 43 (5): 499–517.

———. 2013b. *The New Federal Performance System: Implementing the New GPRA Modernization Act.* Washington, DC: IBM Center for the Business of Government.

Moynihan, Donald P., and Alexander Kroll. 2016. "Performance Management Routines that Work: An Early Assessment of the GPRA Modernization Act." *Public Administration Review* 76 (2): 314–23.

Moynihan, Donald P., and Stéphane Lavertu. 2012. "Does Involvement in Performance Reforms Encourage Performance Information Use? Evaluating GPRA and PART." *Public Administration Review* 72 (4): 592–602.

Posner, Paul L., and Denise Fantone. 2007. "Assessing Federal Program Performance: Observations on the U.S. Office of Management and Budget's Program Assessment Rating Tool and Its Use in the Budget Process." *Public Performance & Management Review* 30: 351–68.

Redburn, F. Steven, and Kathryn Newcomer. 2008. *Achieving Real Improvement in Program performance and Policy Outcomes: The Next Frontier.* Washington, DC: National Academy of Public Administration.

Radin, Beryl. 2006. *Challenging the Performance Movement: Accountability, Complexity, and Democratic Values.* Washington, DC: Georgetown University Press.

Soss, Joe, Richard Fording, and Sanford Schram. 2011. "The Organization of Discipline: From Performance Management to Perversity and Punishment." *Journal of Public Administration Research and Theory* 21(suppl 2): i203–32.

OMB (U.S. Office of Management and Budget). 2001. *The President's Management Agenda.* Washington, DC: Government Printing Office.

———. 2011. *The President's Budget for Fiscal Year 2012: Analytical Perspectives.* Washington, DC: Government Printing Office.

———. 2013a. "Circular A-11." http://www.whitehouse.gov/omb/circulars_a11_current _year_a11_toc.

———. 2013b. "Memorandum to the Heads of Departments and Agencies." M-13-17, July 26. http://www.whitehouse.gov/sites/default/files/omb/memoranda/2013 /m-13-17.pdf.

U.S. Senate Committee on Homeland Security and Governmental Affairs. 2010. *GPRA Modernization Act of 2010.* Washington, DC: U.S. Government Printing Office.

White, Joseph. 2012. "Playing the Wrong PART: The Program Assessment Rating Tool and the Functions of the President's Budget." *Public Administration Review* 72 (1): 112–21.

Winerip, Michael. 2013. "Ex-Schools Chief in Atlanta Is Indicted in Testing Scandal." *New York Times* March 29.

Zients, Jeffery. 2009. "Statement Before the Budget Committee United States Senate." October 29. http://www.whitehouse.gov/sites/default/files/omb/assets/testimony /Zients_102909.pdf.

Country Survey Form

General criteria	Specific questions
Performance information creation	
1. Is there a formal performance budgeting framework?	a) Yes, it applies to all central government Line Ministries and Agencies: b) Yes, but it applies only to Line Ministries c) Yes, but it is optional for Line Ministries and Agencies to abide by d) No, [if it exists] Line Ministries/Agencies have their own performance budgeting frameworks
2. What are the key elements of this standard framework?	Check all that apply a) General guidelines and definitions for the performance budgeting process b) Standard template(s) for reporting performance information back to the CBA c) Standard performance rating system where all programs are graded on a single scale (e.g. effective, ineffective) d) Standard ICT tool/application for entering and reporting performance information to the CBA e) Other:
3. Which institution has overall authority for the design and implementation of the performance framework?	a) Central budget authority b) Ministry of Economy c) Planning Office d) Prime Minister/Presidents Office e) Other
4. Who is responsible for auditing quality of data?	a) Left to agencies themselves b) Supreme audit institution c) Other body:
5. How comprehensive is auditing of performance data?	a) Program managers can expect that their data is audited frequently (every one to three years) b) Program managers can expect that their data will be audited occasionally (less than every seven years, but more than three years) c) Program managers can expect that data is rarely audited
6. Do policymakers trust the data?	a) Yes, policymakers always assume data is reliable and indicative of actual performance b) Mostly, policymakers usually assume data is reliable and indicative of actual performance

table continues next page

Appendix *(continued)*

General criteria	Specific questions
	c) Rarely, policymakers do not usually assume data is reliable and indicative of actual performance
	d) No, policymakers do not have trust in data
7. Are individual ministries/ agencies required to provide performance reports?	a) No b) Yes, on a routine basis specify how frequently: • More frequently than annually • Annually • Less frequently than annually • Not clear how frequently
8. Are individual ministries/ agencies required to provide strategic plans?	a) No b) Yes, on a routine basis specify how frequently: • Every year • Between one and three years • Between three to five years • More than five years • Not clear how frequently
9. Are individual ministries/ agencies required to provide performance targets?	a) No b) Yes
10. Is there a perception that there is too much, too little, or the right amount of data?	a) Policymakers perceive there is more data than is useful b) Policymakers think they have about the right amount of data at their disposal c) Policymakers do not believe there is enough data available to them (If objective measures about the number of performance metrics and how this has changed over time, include in the case description. Please also describe any actions policymakers have taken to manage or increase the volume of data).
11. Do agency heads sign performance agreements?	a) No b) Yes
12. In the presentation of performance data, are current quantitative measures of performance compared to:	a) Performance from previous periods b) Performance against pre-set targets
13. Please indicate which institutions play important roles in generating performance information	a) Chief executive or elected governing body b) Legislature or legislative body c) Central budget authority d) Line ministries e) Agencies f) Civil society organizations g) Other h) Not applicable
14. Does government attempt to measure goals that cut across multiple organizations?	a) No b) Yes, but unclear how each organization contributes to goals c) Yes, with explicit contribution of each organization to the goals

table continues next page

Appendix *(continued)*

General criteria	Specific questions

Performance information dissemination

15. Is performance data provided in budget submissions?
a) In budget submissions to the CBA
b) In budget materials shared with legislatures

16. Is performance information available to the public?
a) Online on Ministry/agency websites
b) Online on central government website
c) Available upon request
d) Not available

System characteristics

17. Connection to Program budget (by program budget, we mean that budget proposals are organized by program area rather than by line item)
Does program budgeting effort exists? Yes/Some/No
If yes, do programs have clearly specified goals? Yes/No
If yes, do program goals align with goals and measures from performance budgeting process? Yes/No

18. Program Evaluation (by program evaluation, we mean a formal effort to estimate if a program is achieving desired goals, which controls for non-governmental factors that lead to performance, such as a randomized control trial)
a) Do formal program evaluations regularly take place across government? Yes/No
If yes, who completes evaluations:
  i. Central budget authority
  ii. Supreme audit institution
  iii. Left to Ministries/agencies
  iv. Other
b) How comprehensive is the practice of project evaluations?
  i. Most programs are evaluated on a regular (3–7 year) basis?
  ii. Some programs are evaluated on a regular basis?
  iii. Programs are rarely, if every, subject to program evaluations
(If there are any objective measures of level of spending or comprehensiveness of program evaluations, please include in case study).
If program evaluations take place, are they linked to discussions of performance?
  i. Yes—discussions of program performance usually integrate both performance data and results of program evaluations
  ii. Some—discussions of program performance sometimes integrate both performance data and results of program evaluations
  iii. No—those who do program evaluations are not connected to those who work with performance measures

19. Connection to multi-year budgeting process (by this we mean a multi-annual budget constraints on sectors or overall government spending, e.g. Medium Term Expenditure Frameworks)
Is there a multi-year budget process in place? Yes/No
Are performance measures included in multi-year spending plans? Yes/No

Performance information use
[Should we specify that all of these questions should be limited to specific sectors?]

20. Are there routines within Ministries/agencies to consider performance goals?
a) No formal requirements to review performance data
b) Yes, there are formal routines to review performance data in detail on annual basis

table continues next page

Appendix *(continued)*

General criteria	*Specific questions*
	c) Yes, there are formal routines to review performance data more frequently than an annual basis (specify how frequently) If yes, please describe these routines:
21. Are there routine discussions of performance between the central budget authority and ministries?	a) No formal requirements to review performance data b) Yes, there are formal routines to review performance data in detail on annual basis c) Yes, there are formal routines to review performance data more frequently than an annual basis (specify how frequently) If yes, please describe these routines:
22. Overall, is performance data used for budgeting purposes?	Which best describes the use of performance data for budget purposes? a) *Presentational performance budgeting*—performance data is included in in budgets, performance reports, or government websites, but there is no clear link to budget decisions b) *Performance-informed budgeting*—performance data is frequently considered in budget decisions, but the relationship is not automatic, and other factors also matter c) *Direct (or formula) performance budgeting*—there is a pre-determined automatic link between level of performance and allocation of resources.
23. Is performance data referred to in budget negotiations between line ministries and central budgetary authority?	a) Always—performance data is regularly discussed in these negotiations b) Usually—performance data is usually discussed in these negotiations c) Rarely—performance data is rarely discussed in these negotiations d) Never
24. How do the Ministries/agencies utilize performance data in their budget negotiations with the central budget authority?	a) Setting allocations for line Ministries/agencies Always/Usually/Rarely/Never b) Setting allocations for specific programs Always/Usually/Rarely/Never c) Reducing spending Always/Usually/Rarely/Never d) Eliminating programs Always/Usually/Rarely/Never e) Increasing spending Always/Usually/Rarely/Never f) Proposing new areas of spending Always/Usually/Rarely/Never g) Developing management reform proposals Always/Usually/Rarely/Never h) Strategic planning/prioritization Always/Usually/Rarely/Never i) Other
25. If performance targets are not met by line ministries/agencies, how likely is it that any of the following consequences are triggered?	a) More intense monitoring of organization and/or program in the Future Always/Usually/Rarely/Never b) Negative consequences for performance evaluations of individuals responsible for program/organization Always/Usually/Rarely/Never

table continues next page

Appendix *(continued)*

General criteria	Specific questions
	c) Organizational or program's poor performance made public Always/Usually/Rarely/Never d) More training provided to staff assigned to program/ organization Always/Usually/Rarely/Never
26. Is performance data used by legislators for accountability purposes?	a) Always—legislative committees regularly use performance data when assessing the performance of Ministries/agencies. b) Usually—legislative committees usually use performance data when assessing the performance of Ministries/agencies. c) Rarely—legislative committees rarely use performance data when assessing the performance of Ministries/agencies. d) Never
27. Overall, is performance data used by managers?	a) Always—managers are very aware of performance data and it routinely influences how they do their job b) Usually—managers are somewhat aware of performance data, and it sometimes influences how they do their job c) Rarely—managers are not very aware of performance data and it generally does not influence how they do their job. d) Never—performance data not seen as relevant to how managers do their job.
28. To what extent do managers make use of performance data in the following activities?	a) Setting program priorities Always/Usually/Rarely/Never b) Allocating resources Always/Usually/Rarely/Never c) Adopting new program approaches or changing work processes Always/Usually/Rarely/Never d) Identifying program problems to be addressed Always/Usually/Rarely/Never e) Taking corrective action to solve problems Always/Usually/Rarely/Never f) Developing or refining new program measures Always/Usually/Rarely/Never g) Setting individual job expectations for employees Always/Usually/Rarely/Never h) Rewarding employees Always/Usually/Rarely/Never
29. Has there been high-profile examples of perverse uses of data	a) No b) Manipulation of data by service providers c) Intense focus on achieving performance targets at the expense of unmeasured aspects of performance (i.e. goal displacement using techniques such as cream-skimming) Please describe:
30. Overall, which groups of actors are most likely to make use of performance data?	a) Program managers b) Central budget officials c) Legislature

Secondary Education—In answering this part of the survey please respond not for the whole of government, but for the secondary school education and its management by the national government. In the case study, please provide specific examples of goals and measures used for secondary education, and it possible, provide links to documentation on these.

table continues next page

Appendix *(continued)*

General criteria	Specific questions
Performance information creation	
31. Do policymakers trust data about the performance of the education system?	a) Yes, policymakers always assume data is reliable and indicative of actual performance b) Mostly, policymakers usually assume data is reliable and indicative of actual performance c) Rarely, policymakers do not usually assume data is reliable and indicative of actual performance d) No, policymakers do not have trust in data
32. Is there a perception that there is too much, too little, or the right amount of data on educational outcomes?	a) Policymakers perceive there is more data than is useful b) Policymakers think they have about the right amount of data at their disposal c) Policymakers believe they do not have enough performance data. (If objective measures of the number of performance metrics for education are available, please include in the case description. Please also describe any actions policymakers have taken to manage or increase the volume of data).
33. In the presentation of education data, are current quantitative measures of performance compared to:	a) Performance from previous periods b) Performance against pre-set targets
34. Is performance data provided in budget submissions?	a) In budget submissions to the CBA b) In budget materials shared with legislatures
35. Is performance information on education available to the public?	a) Online on Ministry/agency websites b) Online on central government website c) Available upon request d) Not available
36. Are there routines within the education Ministry to consider performance goals?	a) No formal requirements to review performance data b) Yes, there are formal routines to review performance data in detail on annual basis c) Yes, there are formal routines to review performance data more frequently than an annual basis (specify how frequently) If yes, please describe these routines:
37. Are there routine discussions of performance between the central budget authority and the education ministry?	a) No formal requirements to review performance data b) Yes, there are formal routines to review performance data in detail on annual basis c) Yes, there are formal routines to review performance data more frequently than an annual basis (specify how frequently) If yes, please describe these routines:
38. Overall, is performance data used for budgeting purposes?	Which best describes the use of performance data for budget purposes in the area of education? a) *Presentational performance budgeting*—performance data is included in in budgets, performance reports, or government websites, but there is no clear link to budget decisions b) *Performance-informed budgeting*—performance data is frequently considered in budget decisions, but the relationship is not automatic, and other factors also matter c) *Direct (or formula) performance budgeting*—there is a pre-determined automatic link between level of performance and allocation of resources.

table continues next page

Appendix *(continued)*

General criteria	Specific questions
39. Is performance data referred to in budget negotiations between the education Ministry and central budgetary authority?	a) Always—performance data is regularly discussed in these negotiations b) Usually—performance data is usually discussed in these negotiations c) Rarely—performance data is rarely discussed in these negotiations d) Never

40. How does the education Ministry utilize performance data in its budget negotiations with the Central budget authority?	a) Setting allocations for line Ministries/agencies
	   Always/Usually/Rarely/Never
	b) Setting allocations for programs
	   Always/Usually/Rarely/Never
	c) Reducing spending
	   Always/Usually/Rarely/Never
	d) Eliminating programs
	   Always/Usually/Rarely/Never
	e) Increasing spending
	   Always/Usually/Rarely/Never
	f) Proposing new areas of spending
	   Always/Usually/Rarely/Never
	g) Developing management reform proposals
	   Always/Usually/Rarely/Never
	h) Strategic planning/prioritization
	   Always/Usually/Rarely/Never
	i) Other

41. If performance targets are not met by the education Ministry, how likely is it that any of the following consequences are triggered?	a) More intense monitoring of organization and/or program in the Future
	   Always/Usually/Rarely/Never
	b) Negative consequences for performance evaluations of individuals responsible for program/organization
	   Always/Usually/Rarely/Never
	c) Organizational or program's poor performance made public
	   Always/Usually/Rarely/Never
	d) More training provided to staff assigned to program/ organization
	   Always/Usually/Rarely/Never

42. Is performance data used by legislators for accountability purposes?	a) Always—legislative committees regularly use performance data when assessing the performance of Ministries/agencies. b) Usually—legislative committees usually use performance data when assessing the performance of Ministries/agencies. c) Rarely—legislative committees rarely use performance data when assessing the performance of Ministries/agencies. d) Never
43. Overall, is performance data used by managers in the education Ministry?	a) Always—managers are very aware of performance data and it routinely influences how they do their job b) Usually—managers are somewhat aware of performance data, and it sometimes influences how they do their job c) Rarely—managers are not very aware of performance data and it generally does not influence how they do their job. d) Never—performance data not seen as relevant to how managers do their job.

table continues next page

Appendix *(continued)*

General criteria	*Specific questions*

44. To what extent do managers in the education Ministry make use of performance data in the following activities?	a) Setting program priorities
	   Always/Usually/Rarely/Never
	b) Allocating resources
	   Always/Usually/Rarely/Never
	c) Adopting new program approaches or changing work processes
	   Always/Usually/Rarely/Never
	d) Identifying program problems to be addressed
	   Always/Usually/Rarely/Never
	e) Taking corrective action to solve problems
	   Always/Usually/Rarely/Never
	f) Developing or refining new program measures
	   Always/Usually/Rarely/Never
	g) Setting individual job expectations for employees
	   Always/Usually/Rarely/Never
	h) Rewarding employees
	   Always/Usually/Rarely/Never

45. Have there been high-profile examples of perverse uses of data in the area of secondary education?	a) No b) Manipulation of data by teachers and principals in schools c) Intense focus on achieving performance targets at the expense of unmeasured aspects of performance (i.e. goal displacement using techniques such as cream-skimming) Please describe:
46. Overall, which groups of actors are most likely to make use of performance data?	a) Managers in the education Ministry b) School officials (e.g. principals) c) Central budget officials d) Legislature